A Dozen Roses
Beautiful Quilts and Pillows

Jennifer Rounds and Catherine Comyns

Martingale®
& COMPANY

A Dozen Roses: Beautiful Quilts and Pillows
© 2007 by Jennifer Rounds and Catherine Comyns

Martingale® & COMPANY That Patchwork Place®

That Patchwork Place® is an imprint of Martingale & Company®.

Martingale & Company
20205 144th Ave. NE
Woodinville, WA 98072-8478 USA
www.martingale-pub.com

Mission Statement

Dedicated to providing quality products and service to inspire creativity.

Credits

President: Nancy J. Martin
CEO: Daniel J. Martin
COO: Tom Wierzbicki
Publisher: Jane Hamada
Editorial Director: Mary V. Green
Managing Editor: Tina Cook
Technical Editor: Darra Williamson
Copy Editor: Melissa Bryan
Design Director: Stan Green
Illustrator: Robin Strobel
Cover and Text Designer: Stan Green
Photographer: Brent Kane

Printed in China
12 11 10 09 08 07   8 7 6 5 4 3 2 1

Library of Congress Cataloging-in-Publication Data
Library of Congress Control Number: 2006026560

ISBN: 978-1-56477-689-1

Dedication

I send my love to Patrick, Max, Parker, and Rambo, an amazingly well-trained quartet of guys who know better than to step on any quilt I have in production on the living room floor. To my parents, B and S, and to my sisters, Patti and Laurie, my thanks and love also; you are always supportive and indulgent of my creative whims.—JCR

To the three roses in my garden: The Prince (John), Peach Blossom (Jen), and Angel Face (Erin)—your sweet bouquet is the delight of my life.—MCMC

Acknowledgments

In creating this book, we acknowledge the work of quiltmakers who have already published rose-making methods in books and patterns. They most definitely have inspired us and sometimes ignited a creative spark. For pieced roses, we bow to Jean Wells and Billy Lauder. Jean kindled the notion of using a log-cabin construction technique to create roses. Billy Lauder has a lovely pieced rose pattern called the "Queen's Rose" that spurred us to experiment with our own pieced roses.

To our friends and quilting companions we send fervent thanks. We are so fortunate to have an abundance of clever friends, each with her own particular talent. Lee Fowler, a longtime friend of Catherine's, put her talents to work and designed a special quilt for us. Laura Nownes perked us up when we were dragging through our protracted conceptual phase. From our as-yet-unnamed quilt/book group, Beate Nellemann took our offbeat inspiration and created an easy project with appeal to fashion-forward teens. Susan Williams set loose her knitting needles and whipped together a pair of squares for the knitted pillow—what took her minutes took Jennifer hours. Kim Butterworth and Valerie Chapla added their special touches to our "Garden Party" quilt. And we cannot forget another pair from our group, Cyndy Rymer (kudos for the "Garden Party" blocks too) and Darra Williamson, extraordinary consultants in the how-tos of creating quilting books. Last, but never least, to Victoria Brown, because you are our delightful English rose.

From Jennifer: I have an acknowledgment for Trish Katz, who set me on this rosy trail a few years ago—it has certainly taken patience and time. Thank you for your support and your contributions to this book. And for my friend Sally Petru, a special thank-you. We've spoken often of collaborating on a project. This book is one step in that effort. Sally is an extraordinary botanical artist ready to transcend full-time mothering and bloom like the flowers she re-creates so wonderfully. And to Catherine, who above all has helped me find the way to graft my little rose idea to her abundant and blooming talents and create this garden of rose projects. I would be a languishing bare-root rose without you.

From Catherine: To quilters from the past for the gifts you have left behind, and to future quilters for inspiring me to do my best. And to Jennifer, for your vision and for inviting me to join you on this adventure.

From both of us: Our most grateful thanks to the Martingale team. We appreciate your enthusiasm as you supported and encouraged us on this journey.

Cont

ents

Introduction

If you have a "thing" for roses, you are in good company; in fact, you are in exalted company. Avid rosarians include ancient Chinese emperors, Ottoman sultans, and Napoleon Bonaparte's first wife, Empress Joséphine. The Romans of classical antiquity were rose-obsessed to an extraordinary degree, carpeting the floors of their homes with petals and suspending petal-filled nets from ceilings to cascade fragrantly upon the heads of guests at the culmination of an evening's festivities. The wealthiest Roman citizens slept on beds of rose petals and bathed in flower-strewn waters. What utter, delightful decadence.

MOST OF US are more modest folk, appreciating roses for their extraordinary beauty, color, and scent. In this book, we want to share our love of roses with you through quiltmaking. Today, more than ever, with the explosion of sewing techniques and technology, re-creating roses with fabric is a wonderful, exciting, and creative adventure. Add incredible fabrics, trims, and beading, and the hardest thing of all is to stop. We've culled our list to 12 projects with a few "quickies" for extra zing.

- *"Spectre de la Rose"* **quilt**. An easy queen-size patchwork quilt in warm tones. This is an updated rendition of the Old Favorite block utilizing a rose-themed fabric.
- *"Spectre de la Rose"* **coordinating knitted pillow**. A drop-dead gorgeous four-patch knitted pillow with a knitted or silk-rose embellishment. There is a bonus pillow sweater for those who can't stop knitting.
- **"French Rose" matelassé and pillow shams.** An easy dimensional-appliqué project, utilizing a purchased matelassé coverlet or matelassé fabric, and coordinating pillow shams.
- **"Velveteen Rose" pillow.** A lush flower made from spirals of rich rose-toned cotton velveteen with a beaded center for a jeweled accent.
- **"Rose-Abunda" sampler quilt.** Traditional rose-themed appliqué blocks interpreted in a whimsical style and featuring a fanciful color scheme. This is a suitable size for wall decor or a throw.
- **"Scottish Rose" throw.** An easy pale blue–and-white patchwork quilt with spiraled rose accents made from bias tape. This is perfect as a throw or baby-sized quilt.
- **"Rose of Havana" quilt.** A small paper-pieced quilt inspired by the beautiful wall tile found in a Colonial Cuban home—a rose quilt with a Caribbean beat. This is an excellent project for a group effort.
- **"Thoroughly Modern Rosie" quilt.** A twin-size quilt utilizing easy patchwork piecing embellished with bias-tape vines and blooming roses. Designed to appeal to the younger, hipper set.
- **"Thoroughly Modern Rosie" bolster pillow.** A bed-width bolster pillow coordinated to match the twin-sized quilt. This is an easy project made from rolled batting, a fabric cover, and rickrack accents.
- **"Bed of Roses" baby quilt.** A project to showcase a rose-themed fabric collection with a bonus rose-petal pillow added for a pretty accent.
- **"Rose and Ribbon Strips" pillow.** An indulgence for trim and luxury-fabric fanatics. Half-yard cuts of delicious rose-themed and floral trims, combined with strips of iridescent silk and beaded accents, create pillow haute couture.
- **"Garden Party" quilt.** A free-style version of the classic log-cabin technique yields dazzling roses. This quilt uses classic New York Beauty arcs to create luscious foliage for op-art roses in three sizes.

We've scattered tips and teasers like rose petals throughout the text to guide and tantalize quiltmakers. Tips are hints and insights that simplify construction. Teasers are suggestions to take the projects to another level of complexity with dazzling results. Do you dare?

Since no other flower can match the story of the rose, *A Dozen Roses* would not be complete without a little rose-related lore, so we've sprinkled some throughout the book as well. The tulip might challenge with tales of Renaissance-era derring-do, but its tale is neither as long, as complex, nor as fragrant as that of the rose. Then there is the visual delight of the rose, which translates beautifully into home decor. From rose-themed fabric to rose-inspired crafts, here is an abundance of great ideas to brighten your home with nature's showiest bloom.

Spectre de la Rose
~ Quilt ~

Lee Fowler—quilt designer, teacher, and Catherine's friend—didn't need to look far for inspiration when we challenged her to make a rose quilt by floating a traditional block on an expanse of rose-patterned fabric. She browsed through the classic Around the Block with Judy Hopkins *(Martingale & Company, 1994) and found that by alternating the Old Favorite block with the Snowball block she had a fully bloomed rose with accent greenery. And by repeating the pattern across a subtle background, she suggests a trellis filled with showy blossoms.*

Once the quilt is complete, you'll want to enhance the project by creating accents for home decor, especially if the quilt is a gift for a special occasion such as a wedding or an anniversary. Try textured accents such as knitted pillows (pages 16 and 19), a striped dupioni silk pillow (page 75), or a "Velveteen Rose" pillow (page 29).

Choosing Fabrics

Auditioning background fabric is very important for this quilt. We tried four different rose-themed fabrics before narrowing the selection to a classic rose-bouquet motif in Italian-country colors. The roses need to dance across the quilt without competing with the theme fabric. A vivid choice will inevitably overwhelm the lacy rose, while insufficient contrast between the accent colors and background fabric will blur the visual effect. Go ahead and sew a trial block or two: the quilt is worth the effort.

Materials

All yardages are based on 42"-wide fabric.

- 8½ yards of floral print for block backgrounds and borders
- 1 yard of dark rose print for Old Favorite blocks
- ⅝ yard of green print #1 for Snowball blocks and flanged inset
- ½ yard of gold print for Old Favorite blocks and inner border
- ⅓ yard of medium-value rose print for Old Favorite blocks*
- ⅓ yard of green print #2 for Old Favorite blocks
- ¼ yard of yellowish orange print for Old Favorite blocks
- ⅞ yard of rust print for binding
- 8⅛ yards of fabric for backing
- 97" x 97" piece of batting

* If you wish, you can use a variety of dark rose prints for a scrappy effect.

Cutting

All measurements include ¼" seam allowances. Cut all strips across the fabric width (selvage to selvage).

From the green print #1, cut:
- 3 strips, 2¼" x 42"; crosscut into 48 squares, 2¼" x 2¼"
- 10 strips, 1¼" x 42"

From the floral print, cut:
- 6 strips, 14½" x 42"; crosscut into 12 squares, 14½" x 14½"
- 7 strips, 2⅝" x 42"; crosscut into 104 squares, 2⅝" x 2⅝". Cut each square once diagonally to yield 208 half-square triangles.
- 12 strips, 4" x 42"; crosscut into 104 rectangles, 2¼" x 4", and 52 squares, 4" x 4"
- 8 strips, 1¼" x 42"
- 10 strips, 10½" x 42"

From the yellowish orange print, cut:
- 2 strips, 2¼" x 42"; crosscut into 32 squares, 2¼" x 2¼"

From the gold print, cut:
- 2 strips, 2¼" x 42"; crosscut into 20 squares, 2¼" x 2¼"
- 8 strips, 1" x 42"

From the dark rose print, cut:
- 3 strips, 4⅜" x 42"; crosscut into 26 squares, 4⅜" x 4⅜". Cut each square once diagonally to yield 52 half-square triangles.
- 2 strips, 4¾" x 42"; crosscut into 13 squares, 4¾" x 4¾". Cut each square twice diagonally to yield 52 quarter-square triangles.

From the green print #2, cut:
- 4 strips, 2¼" x 42"; crosscut into 52 squares, 2¼" x 2¼"

From the medium-value rose print, cut:
- 2 strips, 4" x 42"; crosscut into 13 squares, 4" x 4"

From the rust print, cut:
- 10 strips, 2½" x 42"

Making the Snowball Blocks

You will make 12 Snowball blocks for this quilt.

1. Draw a diagonal line on the wrong side of each 2¼" green #1 square.
2. With right sides together, pin a green #1 square to each corner of a 14½" floral square. Sew directly on the drawn line. Trim the seams to ¼"; press. Make 12 Snowball blocks.

Draw line.   Sew.

 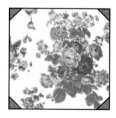

Trim.   Make 12.

Making the Old Favorite Blocks

You will make 13 Old Favorite blocks for this quilt in two different fabric combinations: eight of block A and five of block B.

Designed and machine quilted by Lee Fowler. Pieced by Catherine Comyns.

Finished Quilt: 93" x 93" • **Finished Block: 14" x 14"**

1. Sew two floral triangles to each 2¼" gold and yellowish orange square as shown; press. Make 52.

2. Sew a 4⅜" dark rose half-square triangle to a yellowish orange/floral unit from step 1 as shown; press. Make 32 and label these *block A*. Repeat using 4⅜" dark rose half-square triangles and gold/floral units. Make 20 and label these *block B*.

Block A.
Make 32.

Block B.
Make 20.

3. Sew two floral triangles to each 4¾" dark rose quarter-square triangle to make a flying-geese unit as shown; press. Make 52.

Make 52.

4. Sew two 2¼" green #2 squares, two 2¼" x 4" floral rectangles, and one flying-geese unit from step 3 together as shown; press. Make 26.

Make 26.

5. Sew two 2¼" x 4" floral rectangles, two matching units from step 2, and one 4" floral square together as shown; press. Make 26 total.

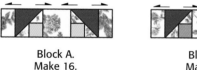

Block A.
Make 16.

Block B.
Make 10.

6. Sew two flying-geese units from step 3, two 4" floral squares, and one 4" medium-value rose square together as shown; press. Make 13.

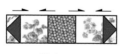

Make 13.

7. Arrange and sew two units from step 4, two matching units from step 5, and one unit from step 6 as shown; press. Make 13 total Old Favorite blocks.

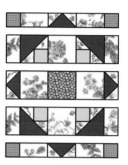

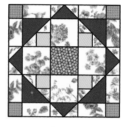

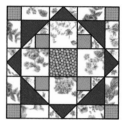

Block A.
Make 8.

Block B.
Make 5.

Assembling the Quilt Top

1. Sew two Snowball blocks and three Old Favorite blocks together, alternating them as shown; press. Make two rows with two Old Favorite A blocks and one Old Favorite B block. Make one row with three Old Favorite B blocks.

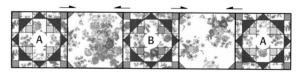

Make 2.

Make 1.

2. Sew two Old Favorite A blocks and three Snowball blocks together, alternating them as shown; press. Make two rows.

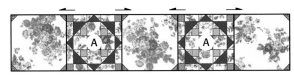

Make 2.

3. Sew the rows from steps 1 and 2 together, alternating them as shown; press.

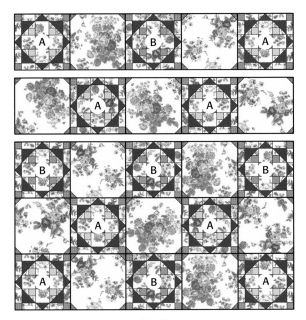

Assembly diagram

Attaching the Inner Border

1. Sew the 1¼" x 42" floral strips together end to end. Press the seams open. From this long strip, cut four strips, each 75" long. Repeat using the 1" x 42" gold strips.

Border Variation

For a touch of sparkle, piece random bits of leftover orange scraps at various spots throughout the gold border.

2. With right sides together, sew a floral strip to a gold strip along the long edges. Press the seam toward the gold strip. Make four inner-border units.

3. Fold one inner-border unit in half, finger-press, and pin-mark the midpoint. Measure the quilt top through the center from top to bottom, and divide by two. Measure this distance from each side of the midpoint of the inner-border unit and mark with a pin. Repeat to make a second side-border unit.

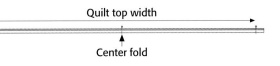

Quilt top width

Center fold

4. Fold the quilt top in half vertically and horizontally and pin-mark the midpoints on each side. Pin a marked inner-border unit from step 3 to one side of the quilt top, matching the midpoints and the outer pins to the corners of the quilt top. (The ends of the border will extend beyond the corners of the quilt top.) Sew the border to the quilt top, starting and stopping with a backstitch ¼" from the corners. Press the seams toward the border unit. Repeat for the opposite side of the quilt top.

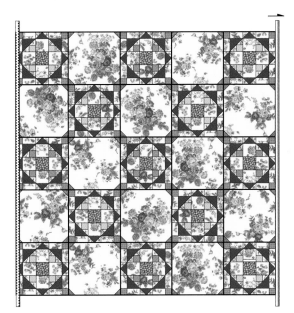

5. Measure the quilt top through the center from side to side, including the inner-border units you just added. Measure, pin, and sew a remaining pin-marked inner-border unit to the top and bottom of the quilt top. (Remember: the ends of the borders will extend beyond the quilt top.)

6. Place the quilt top right side up on a clean, flat surface with one border extension overlapping the adjacent border. Be sure the entire quilt top is supported so that its weight doesn't drag and distort the corner. Fold under and pin the end of the overlapping border at a 45° angle, using a ruler with angle markings as a guide. Check that the corner of the border is an accurate 90° angle; press.

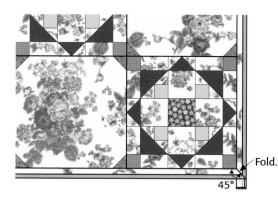

7. Mark the unfolded border end along the pressed edge as shown.

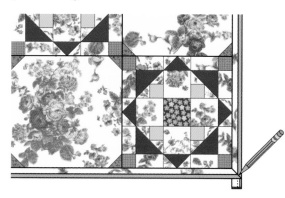

8. Trim the pressed (overlapping) border ¼" from the pressed edge. Trim the marked (overlapped) border ¼" from the marked line. Pin the trimmed border ends right sides together. Beginning at the point where the border seams meet, stitch from the inner corner to the outer corner of the border. Press the seam open. Repeat for the three remaining corners.

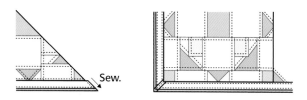

Attaching the Outer Border

1. Sew the 1¼" x 42" green #1 strips together end to end. Press the seams open. Fold and press the strip in half lengthwise, wrong sides together, to make the inset flange. Sew the 10½" x 42" floral border strips together end to end; press.

2. Measure the quilt top through the center from top to bottom. Cut two green #1 inset flanges and two 10½"-wide floral borders to this measurement.

3. Using a scant ¼" seam, baste a trimmed green #1 inset flange to the inner edge of a floral border. Repeat for the second side border.

4. Referring to "Attaching Borders" on page 90, sew the border units from step 3 to the sides of the quilt top. Press the seams toward the inner borders.

5. Measure the quilt top through the center from side to side between the outer borders. Cut two green #1 inset flanges to this measurement plus 1". Turn the ends of each flange ½" to the wrong side and press. Fold the strips in half lengthwise, wrong sides together; press.

6. Measure the quilt top through the center from side to side including the outer borders. Cut two 10½"-wide floral borders to this measurement.

7. Fold one floral border from step 6 and one green #1 inset flange from step 5 in half and mark the midpoints. Pin the flange to the floral border, matching the midpoints. The ends of the floral border will extend beyond the flanged border. Using a scant ¼" seam, baste a trimmed flange to the inner edge of a floral border. Make two. Pin and sew the border units to the top and bottom of the quilt top; press.

Finishing the Quilt

Refer to "Quiltmaking Basics" on page 88 for guidance in layering, basting, and quilting the quilt top. Lee used an allover floral design to machine quilt *"Spectre de la Rose."* Use the 2½"-wide rust strips to bind the quilt, and finish by adding a sleeve and label.

The Delicate and Fleeting Fragance of A Rose

Le Spectre de la Rose is a ballet originally choreographed for Vaslav Nijinsky, arguably the greatest male dancer of his generation, and is based on a lovely poem of the same name by Frenchman Théophile Gautier. Dressing a man in rose petals to dance in the role of a flower's spirit was wholly unexpected, even incongruous, but apparently Nijinsky was so profoundly gifted a performer that he could embody, through the union of movement and music, something as amorphous as the delicate and fleeting fragrance of a rose. Each night of a performance, the wardrobe mistress would sew rose petals into his cap and tights; perhaps it was that transforming scent that gave him the power to enchant the audience.

Spectre de la Rose
~ Coordinating Knitted Pillow ~

Designed and knitted by Catherine Comyns, Jennifer Rounds, and Susan Williams

Finished Pillow: 16" x 16"

This pillow project is for those who have been bitten by the knitting bug and want a quick, high-impact project for home decor. (After all, how many scarves can a novice knit?) Sew four garter-stitch squares together into a quilter's Four Patch block, set the knitted block on point, grab a pillow form, pull the four corners to the center, and stitch the seams closed. Knit a rose for the center or, if you enjoy ribbon art, make a silk-rose accent.

Textured fabric is a rising trend in interior design and this pillow adds a delicious nubbly quality to a pillow ensemble. If this project doesn't fully satisfy your knitting urge, make our bonus pillow sweater too.

Materials

- **Yarn A:** approximately 150 yards of Katia Flash Print, color 805, or other variegated caramel chunky-weight yarn for pillow
- **Yarn B:** approximately 150 yards of Linie 87 Street, color 08, or other variegated copper chunky-weight yarn for pillow
- **Yarn C:** approximately 30 yards of variegated pink chunky-weight yarn for rose
- **Yarn D:** approximately 15 yards of green worsted-weight yarn for leaves
- Straight knitting needles, size 9
- 2 double-pointed needles, size 9
- Yarn needle
- 6" circle of tulle
- 16" x 16" pillow form

Knitting the Pillow

Gauge isn't important for this project because knitted fabric is very forgiving. Aim for approximately three stitches per inch. For how-to help, refer to any basic knitting instruction book. Skills needed for this project include knitting and purling, increasing and decreasing stitches, binding off, and making I-cord.

1. With yarn A, cast on 30 stitches. Knit every row until the piece is a square, approximately 10" x 10". Bind off and set aside. Make two squares with yarn A.

2. Repeat step 1 to make two squares with yarn B.

3. Use the yarn needle to stitch each yarn A square to a yarn B square as shown. Note that the squares are placed so that the stitching in each square runs at a 90° angle (perpendicular) to its neighboring squares.

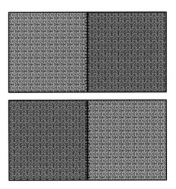

4. Arrange and stitch the two units from step 3 together to make a square as shown.

5. Bring the outside corners together and stitch toward the inside corners.

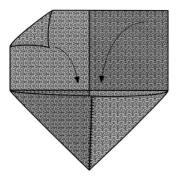

6. Insert the pillow form and stitch the center opening closed.

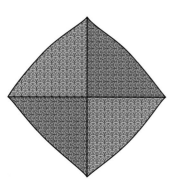

Knitting the Accent Rose and Leaves

1. Using the two double-pointed needles and yarn C, cast on six stitches and knit 30" of I-cord. Bind off. Coil the I-cord into a rose shape and stitch to the tulle circle. Trim any excess tulle.

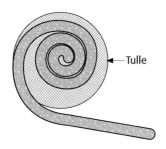

2. Using yarn D and the straight knitting needles, cast on three stitches. Proceed as follows to make a leaf:

- **Row 1:** K1 stitch; YO (increase); K1; YO; K1.
- **Row 2 and all wrong-side rows:** Purl.
- **Row 3:** K2; YO; K1; YO; K2.
- **Row 5:** K3; YO; K1; YO; K3.
- **Row 7:** K4; YO; K1; YO; K4.
- **Row 9:** Knit across.
- **Row 11:** K3; ssk (decrease); K1; K2tog (decrease); K3.
- **Row 13:** K2; ssk; K1; K2tog; K2.
- **Row 15:** K1; ssk; K1; K2tog; K1.
- **Row 17:** Ssk; K1; K2tog.
- **Row 19:** K3tog.

Cut the yarn and pull the end through the last stitch to secure.

3. Repeat step 2 to make a total of three leaves.
4. Pin the rose to the center of the pillow. Arrange and pin the three leaves around the rose. Stitch the leaves, and then the rose, in place.

Bonus Pillow Sweater

Designed and made by Catherine Comyns

You'll love this easy project! Buy one skein of a fancy yarn and some coordinating decorative ribbons, or use leftovers from another project. Check the gauge note on the yarn label to guide you in selecting the proper needle size and to determine how many stitches per inch those needles will yield. If the label says 16 stitches per 4 inches and you want a 15" x 15" pillow sweater, do a little simple math: 16 stitches per 4" = 4 stitches per 1" (16 ÷ 4), so for a 15" x 15" pillow, cast on 60 stitches (15 x 4).

Knit until the square equals your target measurement, and then bind off all the stitches. Cover a pillow form with a favorite fabric, and place the form on point in the center of the pillow "sweater." Bring the sweater corners to the center, thread decorative ribbon(s) through the corners, and tie into a big bow to fasten the sweater closed.

Make pillow cover.

Insert pillow form.
Stitch closed.

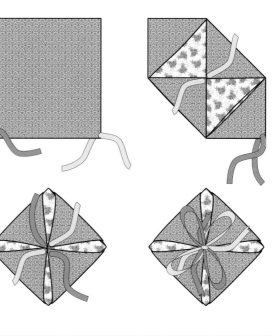

French Rose
~ Matelassé Coverlet and Pillow Shams ~

I adapted a lyrical French rose pattern drawn by botanical artist Sally Petru to create the look of a classic floral appliqué coverlet without a huge investment of time. The key element is a purchased matelassé coverlet. A matelassé coverlet is a machine-washable, user-friendly woven cotton coverlet (often a Portuguese import) that is available in white, cream, or pastel tones and a full range of mattress sizes.

Look in catalogs, bed-and-bath shops, or online to find a matelassé coverlet with a pattern and texture you like—the pattern will mimic the look of hand quilting for the background of your quilt. Frequently the matelassé coverlet will be paired with a set of matching pillow shams. Use them if you wish, or cut down a twin-size matelassé coverlet to make your own shams. As an alternative, some national fabric chains carry matelassé yardage.—Jennifer

Create an Ensemble
This project is an ideal bridal or anniversary gift, with all the beauty of an heirloom quilt but half the fuss! Spice things up with coordinating pillowcases and sheets. Select them in shades to blend with your coverlet fabrics, or make your own bed linens from purchased fabric.

Materials

All yardages are based on 42"-wide fabric unless otherwise noted.

▸ 1 queen-size purchased matelassé coverlet
▸ 2 purchased matching pillow shams or 3⅜ yards of 54"-wide matelassé fabric
▸ 2⅜ yards *total* of assorted rose-colored prints in a wide range of values for rose appliqués and binding*
▸ 2½ yards *total* of assorted green prints for stems and leaf appliqués
▸ ⅝ yard of peach print for accent-band appliqué
▸ ⅛ yard *total* of assorted yellow prints for rose appliqués
▸ Template material
▸ ¼" and ¾" bias-tape makers
▸ Fabric marking pen or pencil
▸ Large piece of flat cardboard
▸ #8 Between needle for appliqué
▸ #11 embroidery needles with elongated eyes for decorative stitching
▸ 3 skeins of embroidery floss in varied yellow tones
▸ 4 decorative buttons, 1" diameter (optional)
▸ Chopstick or stiletto

*If you prefer to keep the existing bound edge of the matelassé coverlet, reduce this yardage to 1⅝ yards.

Cutting

All measurements include ¼" seam allowances. Cut all strips across the fabric width (selvage to selvage) unless otherwise noted. Refer to "Cutting with Templates" on page 88 for instructions on cutting appliqué shapes. Patterns for pieces A through E appear on page 28.

From the assorted green prints, cut a *total* of:
▸ 282 of piece A
▸ 100 rectangles, 1¼" x 2½"
▸ 50 of piece B
▸ 50 rectangles, ¾" x 1¼"
▸ ½"-wide bias strips to total approximately 400"

From the assorted rose-colored prints, cut a *total* of:
▸ 38 of piece C
▸ 262 of piece D
▸ 10 strips, 2½" x 42", for binding (optional)

From the yellow prints, cut a *total* of:
▸ 38 of piece E

From the peach print, cut:
▸ 1½"-wide bias strips to total approximately 300"

From the optional matelassé fabric for shams, cut:
▸ 2 rectangles, 27" x 34"
▸ 4 rectangles, 23" x 27"

Preparing the Faced Appliqué Pieces

Facing the appliqué pieces creates the illusion of depth against the denser matelassé fabric.

Create Visual Interest

Mix up patterns, tones, and values when sewing together the blossom and leaf tops and backs. Variations add visual interest when the edges are folded back for leaf, rosebuds, and sepal accents.

Solid Leaves

Pin two A pieces right sides together. Use a small machine stitch to sew ⅛" from the cut edge all around the leaf shape. Cut a small slit in the leaf back, taking care not to cut through to the leaf front. Turn the leaf right side out, using a chopstick or stiletto to smooth the shape; press. Make 91.

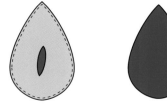

Make 91.

Floral design based on original art by Sally Petru (art shown below; used with permission).
Coverlet and shams appliquéd by Jennifer Rounds

Finished Coverlet: 84" x 94" • Finished Pillow Shams: 26" x 33"

Split Leaves

1. Use a ¼" seam allowance to sew together two 1¼" x 2½" assorted green rectangles along their long sides. Press the seam open. Make 50.

Make 50.

2. Use template A to cut 50 split leaves from the step 1 units. Referring to "Solid Leaves" on page 22, use the split leaves and assorted A pieces to complete 50 faced split leaves.

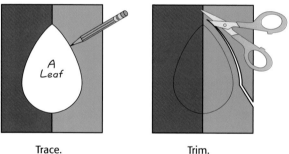

Trace.   Trim.

Inset Leaves

1. Pin a ¾" x 1¼" green rectangle right side up to the wrong side of a different-colored green B piece. Use your preferred method to appliqué the slit in the B piece to the green rectangle as shown. Trim the excess fabric from the wrong side of the rectangle, leaving a scant ¼"-wide seam. Make 50.

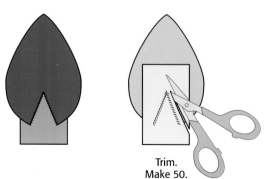

Trim.
Make 50.

2. Referring to "Solid Leaves" on page 22, use the appliquéd units from step 1 and the remaining A pieces to complete 50 faced inset leaves.

Solid, split, and inset leaves

Rose Bases

Pin two C pieces right sides together. Use a small machine stitch to sew ⅛" from the cut edge all around the base shape. Cut a small slit in the rose base back, taking care not to cut through to the rose base front. Turn the rose base right side out using a chopstick or stiletto to smooth the shape; press. Make 19.

Petals and Rose Centers

Referring to "Rose Bases" above, use the assorted D pieces to complete 131 faced petals. Use the assorted E pieces to complete 19 rose centers.

Making the Bias Accent and Stems

Referring to "Making Folded Bias Strips" on page 89 and the manufacturer's instructions for the bias-tape maker, make approximately 400" of ¼"-wide folded bias strips using the ½"-wide green bias strips and approximately 300" of ¾"-wide folded bias strips using the 1½"-wide peach bias strips. Coil the folded strips around a cardboard tube until needed.

Placing the Appliqués on the Coverlet

For this phase of the process, place the large piece of cardboard between the mattress and the coverlet to serve as a firm surface for pinning the appliqué shapes in place. Shift the cardboard as needed while pinning. A dinner or salad plate is useful for shaping the curved accent band.

1. Spread the prewashed matelassé coverlet on a large, flat surface, preferably the intended bed or one of equal size. Arrange the edges to hang evenly on all sides.
2. Pin the ¾"-wide peach folded bias strips to the coverlet in gentle curves along the mattress edge. Start at the head of the bed and work toward the foot. Turn and follow the foot to the other side of the bed, and then turn again and run the band back to the head of the bed. When you are satisfied with the arrangement, baste the band in place. Make the basting stitches extra long so the rose stems can slide under the accent band later.

Rose Blossoms

This project features three types of rose blossoms: front view, side view, and rosebud. You will make a total of 12 front-view roses, 7 side-view roses, and 12 rosebuds for the coverlet and pillow shams.

A front-view rose has a yellow center and five petals arranged on a flower base.

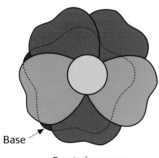

Base

Front-view rose

A side-view rose has a partial view of a yellow center, a folded flower base, and three to five petals.

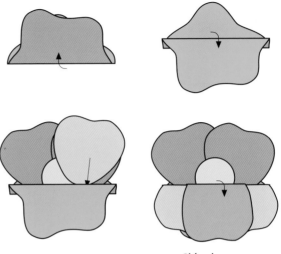

Side-view rose

A rosebud has two to three folded petals nestled within two folded leaves.

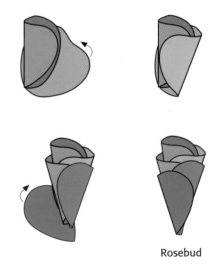

Rosebud

Use the complete width of the ¼"-wide green folded bias strips for the main stems and rose stems. To create the delicate leaf stems, fold the ¼"-wide strip in half lengthwise to make a strip ⅛" wide. A light pressing of the creased bias strip will help maintain the fold.

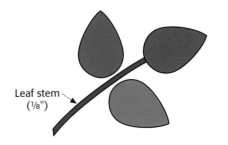

Leaf stem (⅛")

1. Sort and pin the rose bases, petals, and rose centers into sets for the front-view and side-view roses. Pair the petals and leaves for the rosebuds.

2. Referring to the photo on page 23, arrange nine front-view and five side-view roses on the coverlet. Weave stems over and under the peach accent band to reach the roses. When you are satisfied with the arrangement, pin in place.

3. Referring to the photo, fill in the design with 10 rosebuds, 134 leaves, and assorted leaf stems; pin in place.

Stitching the Appliqués

Work with short lengths of thread (such as 12" to 15") to minimize the fraying that results from repeated piercings of the heavy matelassé fabric. Select thread color to match the appliqués. Keep in mind that roses are thorny and so there is a little more freedom for stitches to show.

This is not the time to use a delicate #12 straw needle for appliqué. A workhorse #8 Between is sharp and strong—essential qualities for plowing through the densely woven cotton of the matelassé coverlet. For decorative stitching, use the #11 embroidery needles.

1. Working in small sections, use your preferred method to appliqué a section of the accent band in place; next stitch the rose stems and leaf stems. Finish each section by stitching the roses, rosebuds, and leaves in place. Spread out the coverlet occasionally to check placement and alignment.

2. Use yellow embroidery floss and a #11 embroidery needle to add French knots and backstitches for the stamen accents.

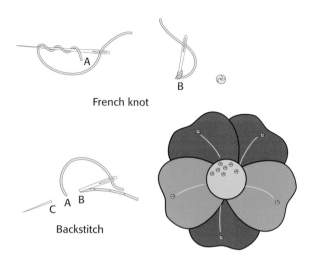

French knot

Backstitch

Finishing the Coverlet

Chances are that a purchased matelassé coverlet will have a decorative finished edge. Keep it as is or bind the coverlet with the 2½"-wide assorted rose strips. (Stay stitch the edges of the coverlet just inside the planned cutting line before you remove the existing bound edge. Once cut, the unprotected edges of a matelassé coverlet are apt to ripple.) Refer to "Quiltmaking Basics" on page 88 for guidance in preparing and adding the binding and label.

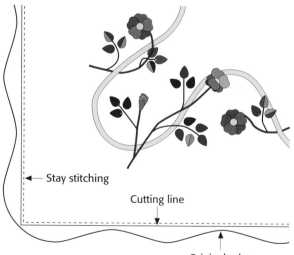

Stay stitching

Cutting line

Original edge

Finishing the Pillow Shams

Purchased pillow shams require very little finishing aside from adding the appliquéd embellishments. Referring to the photo on page 21, arrange the main stems and the rose and leaf stems, as well as the remaining front-view roses, side-view roses, leaves, and rosebuds on the shams; pin. Use your preferred method to appliqué the elements in place.

Adding Embellishment

Adding decorative buttons and trimming the edges with accent binding to match the coverlet are easy and pretty options for dressing up your appliquéd shams.

1. To make your own pillow shams, follow the coverlet directions to appliqué the stems, roses, and leaves to each 27" x 34" matelassé fabric rectangle.

2. Fold ¼" to the wrong side along one 27" edge of each 23" x 27" matelassé rectangle; stitch.

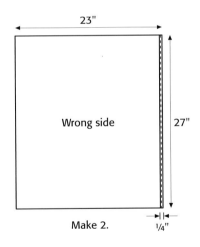

23"

Wrong side

27"

Make 2.   ¼"

3. Fold the hemmed edge under again, this time 2", on two 23" x 27" units from step 2; pin. Topstitch 1¾" and ¼" from the folded edge.

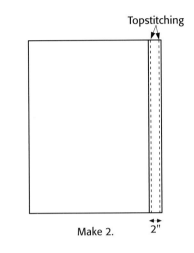

Topstitching

Make 2.   2"

4. Place a pin at the center of the finished edge of each unit from step 3. Mark two buttonholes in each unit, one 5" above and one 5" below the pin. Remove the pin and make buttonholes to fit the selected buttons.

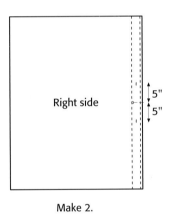

Right side   5"
5"

Make 2.

Rose Legend

The French rose, or *Rosa gallica*, is an original rose with a legendary past. One version, a semi-double red blossom called the "Apothecary's Rose," is the medieval medicinal rose. These roses, with their opened petals and golden centers, also became religious and imperial symbols. The white *Rosa alba* symbolized the Virgin Mary and later, during the fabled War of the Roses in England, the House of York took that rose as its own while the rival Lancastrians took a red *Rosa gallica* as their emblem. Only a wedding between the warring houses resolved the bitterness: Henry Tudor (Henry VII) married Elizabeth of York, creating a new royal line and the "Tudor Rose," a white rose in the center of a red one. That alliance also yielded that scourge of wives, Henry VIII.

5. Place one of the appliquéd sham fronts, right side up, on a clean, flat surface. Place a unit from step 4 and then a unit from step 3 wrong side up over the sham front, aligning the raw edges as shown. (The units will overlap at the center.) Use a ½" seam allowance to sew around the perimeter of the sham. Repeat for the second sham.

6. Turn the shams right side out, clipping the corners as needed. Press lightly to flatten the edges.

7. Open the buttonholes and mark the pillow-sham backs for button placement. Stitch the buttons in place.

8. Sew 3" from the edges of the band to make a flanged border on each sham.

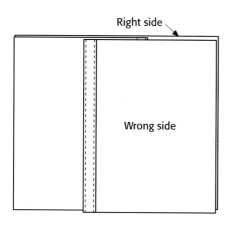

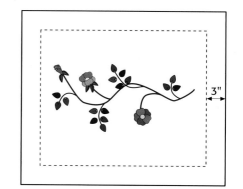

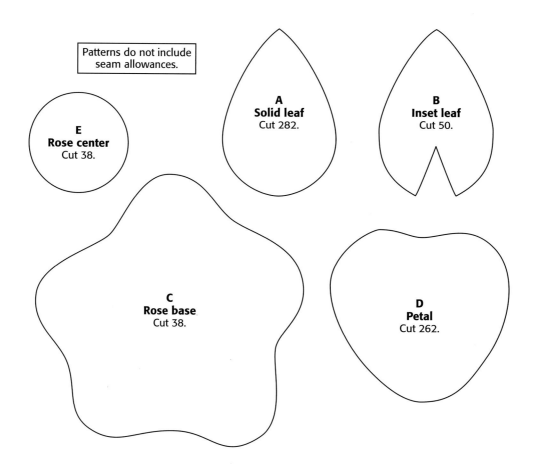

Patterns do not include seam allowances.

E
Rose center
Cut 38.

A
Solid leaf
Cut 282.

B
Inset leaf
Cut 50.

C
Rose base
Cut 38.

D
Petal
Cut 262.

Velveteen Rose
~ Pillow ~

Designed and made by Jennifer Rounds

Finished Pillow: 12" diameter

There is something quite wonderful about cupping a fully opened rose and inhaling its fragrance. Growing up in humid Florida, where the bugs and climate are so hard on large-scale efforts, I had few opportunities to savor the colors, scents, and textures of roses grown in formal gardens. I had a rose epiphany when I was a college student on my first trip to England and found an extraordinary collection of roses in a retreat called Queen Mary's Garden in London's Regent's Park. That was the beginning of a year of rose wonders— I could not believe how virtually everyone with a spot of earth in the UK grew roses so effortlessly. This velveteen pillow recalls those times when I paused in a garden to trace the whorls of a petal-heavy blossom, absorbing a hint of its perfume on my fingertip.—*Jennifer*

Materials

All yardages are based on 42"-wide fabric.

- 1½ yards of velveteen in a rose-inspired color such as red, pink, or peach for pillow back and petals
- ½ yard of cotton fabric to match the rose-colored velveteen
- ¼ yard of green velveteen for leaves
- ⅛ yard of stabilizer, such as Timtex
- Fine-point permanent marking pen
- 50 to 100 *total* of 10/0 beads in assorted reds, oranges, and yellows for rose center
- Polyester fiberfill
- Chopstick or stiletto

Cutting

All measurements include ¼" seam allowances. Refer to "Cutting with Templates" on page 88 for instructions on cutting the leaves. The pattern for the leaf (fabric and stabilizer) appears on page 31.

From the cotton fabric, cut:
- 1 circle, 2" diameter
- 1 circle, 12½" diameter

From the rose-colored velveteen, cut:
- 1 circle, 12½" diameter; save scraps for strips
- 4"-wide to 6"-wide bias strips to total 200"

From the green velveteen, cut:
- 4 leaves

From the stabilizer, cut:
- 2 leaves*

*Note the special cutting lines for the stabilizer.

Assembling the Pillow

1. Fold the 2" cotton circle into quarters. Find the center and use it as the starting point for beading. Bead a circle approximately ¾" in diameter, alternating and clustering the red, orange, and yellow beads to mimic the look of a rose's center.

2. Fold the 12½" cotton circle into quarters and place a small mark on the outermost edges of the folds. These are the pinning guides for sewing the pillow top to the pillow back.

3. Pin the beaded circle to the center of the 12½" cotton circle and baste in place. For an asymmetrical rose, place the beaded circle off center.

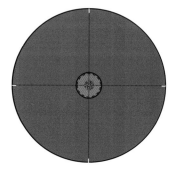

4. With wrong sides together, fold the rose-colored bias strips in half lengthwise. Use matching thread to baste ¼" from the raw edges of the folded strips.

Baste raw edges together.

5. Cut two 3" lengths from the narrowest rose-colored bias strip and pin them to the 12½" cotton circle surrounding the beaded circle. Manipulate the fabric so it cups and reveals the beads. Stitch the strips to the cotton circle.

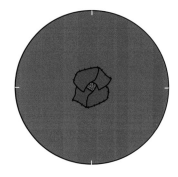

6. Continue pinning and stitching rose-colored bias strips in an ever-enlarging circle around the beaded center, overlapping the end of the prior strip with each addition. Anticipate the

outer edge of the circle: the last rows of petals should be sewn to the edge of the cotton circle. Make adjustments by widening or tightening the last few spirals. Trim the excess fabric.

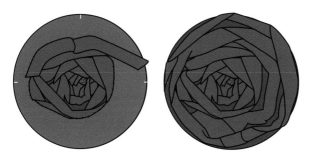

Listen to the Fabric

Let the fabric dictate curvature: Do not stretch the bias strips out of shape with a tight fit or reveal stitching lines with loose placement. Roses have glorious curves, so soften sharp angles and make rounded folds. Take advantage of the tendency of the fabric to pleat as it adjusts to the curves; those pleats and folds enhance the rose-petal effect.

7. Pin two fabric leaves right sides together. Use a small machine stitch to sew ¼" from the cut edge, leaving the bottom edge open for inserting the stabilizer. Turn the leaf right side out, using a chopstick or stiletto to smooth the shape. Make two.

8. Insert a stabilizer leaf inside each unit from step 7, adjusting the fit so the leaves are flat. Machine stitch the leaf veins and trim the threads.

9. Arrange and pin the leaves on the finished pillow top. Baste in place, matching the raw edges.

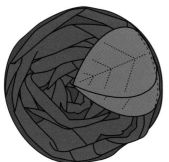

10. Fold the 12½" rose-colored velveteen circle into quarters and mark the folds at the outer edges on the wrong side of the fabric. Match those marks with the marks made on the 12½" cotton circle in step 2. Pin, easing the fit as needed.

11. Working from the velveteen side, sew ¼" from the raw edge of the circle, leaving an opening for turning. Turn the pillow right side out; stuff. Sew the opening closed with invisible hand stitches.

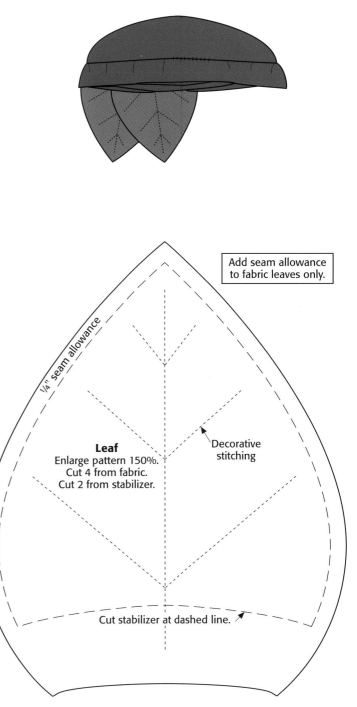

Add seam allowance to fabric leaves only.

¼" seam allowance

Leaf
Enlarge pattern 150%.
Cut 4 from fabric.
Cut 2 from stabilizer.

Decorative stitching

Cut stabilizer at dashed line.

Rose-Abunda
~ Sampler Quilt ~

I consider myself a traditional quilter and, although I may machine piece quilt blocks, I favor hand appliqué and hand quilting. I have even been known to enjoy a bit of hand piecing, too. My inspiration comes from studying antique quilts in books and museums, learning from their color arrangements and sometimes offbeat interpretations of design motifs, such as flowers.

The variety of rose-themed blocks has always intrigued me; some of them bear little resemblance to what I would call a rose. With "Rose-Abunda," I wanted to make a sampler of rose blocks tweaked to a more uniform rose shape. Back in 2004, I took my idea-in-the-works to a class with Sue Benner at an Empty Spools seminar in Pacific Grove, California. Sue encouraged me to go for an abundant and bountiful look. Gwen Marston also weighed in with her support and example. She, too, is an unabashed quilting traditionalist and an advocate of those who enjoy making their own interpretations of classic blocks.

Stitching this sampler of rose blocks was a joy for me—an experience I relive daily when I wake and see this lovely quilt on my bedroom wall.—Catherine

Choosing Fabric
I used a multicolored Kaffe Fassett plaid as the focal fabric for selecting the coordinating appliqué fabrics. Then, to carry the plaid through to the appliqué design, I used touches of that fabric in the blocks. To achieve the same look, cut all the prairie-point squares from the focus fabric first and then cut selected appliqué shapes from the remaining focus fabric.

Materials

All yardages are based on 42"-wide fabric.

- ▶ 4 yards of pale pink print for blocks, setting triangles, and borders*
- ▶ 2½ yards *total* of assorted green solids for appliqué
- ▶ 2⅛ yards *total* of assorted pink, purple, and orange solids for appliqué
- ▶ 1⅜ yards of multicolored plaid for appliqué and prairie points
- ▶ ¼ yard of gold solid for appliqué
- ▶ 3½ yards of fabric for backing
- ▶ 63" x 63" piece of batting
- ▶ ¼" and ½" bias-tape makers
- ▶ Template material

* Use 2 or 3 different prints if you wish.

Cutting

All measurements include ¼" seam allowances. Cut all strips across the fabric width (selvage to selvage) unless otherwise noted. Refer to "Cutting with Templates" on page 88 for instructions on cutting appliqué shapes. Patterns for pieces A through L appear on pages 38–41.

From the *lengthwise grain* of the pale pink print, cut:
- ▶ 2 strips, 9" x 41½"
- ▶ 2 strips, 9" x 58½"

From the remaining pale pink print, cut:
- ▶ 5 squares, 16" x 16"*
- ▶ 1 square, 21¾" x 21¾"; cut twice diagonally to yield 4 quarter-square triangles
- ▶ 2 squares, 11⅛" x 11⅛"; cut each square once diagonally to yield 2 half-square triangles (4 total)

From the assorted green solids, cut a *total* of:
- ▶ 1"-wide bias strips to total approximately 400"
- ▶ 4 bias strips, ½" x 6"
- ▶ 2 bias strips, ½" x 5"
- ▶ 34 of piece B
- ▶ 214 of piece G
- ▶ 6 of piece I

*These squares are cut oversized and will be trimmed when the appliqué is complete.

Designed and made by Catherine Comyns

Finished Quilt: 58½" x 58½" plus prairie points

Finished Block: 14½" x 14½"

From the assorted pink, purple, and orange solids, cut a *total* of:
- ▶ 40 of piece A
- ▶ 10 of piece C
- ▶ 38 of piece D
- ▶ 38 of piece E
- ▶ 1 of piece K

From the gold solid, cut:
- ▶ 38 of piece F

From the multicolored plaid, cut:
- ▶ 8 strips, 4" x 42"; crosscut into 72 squares, 4" x 4"
- ▶ 4 bias strips, ½" x 10"
- ▶ 2 of piece H
- ▶ 1 of piece J
- ▶ 1 of piece L

Preparing for Appliqué

1. Fold and press each 16" pink square in half vertically and horizontally; unfold. Refold each square on both diagonals and press again, taking care not to flatten the previous

creases. You will use these pressed lines as registers for placing the appliqué shapes.

2. Lightly draw a line ¾" from the outside edges of each pink square. This line marks the seam line for the block. Be sure to keep all appliqué shapes within the boundaries of these drawn lines.

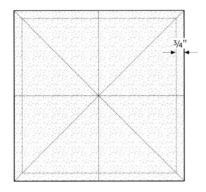

3. Referring to "Making Folded Bias Strips" on page 89 and the package instructions for the bias-tape maker, make four ¼" x 6" folded bias strips and two ¼" x 5" folded bias strips using the ½"-wide green bias strips; four ¼" x 10" folded bias strips using the ½"-wide plaid bias strips; and approximately 400" of ½"-wide folded bias strips using the 1"-wide green bias strips.

Appliquéing the Blocks

The patterns provided are suitable for traditional hand appliqué. Fans of fusible appliqué can reverse and adapt the patterns to suit fusible web.

Each block is accompanied by a block diagram. Stitch the appliqué shapes in the order indicated in the block instructions. Press the completed blocks carefully and trim to measure 15" square.

Plan Ahead

Consider building the roses before stitching them to the block. Appliqué a smaller shape to a larger one and, from the back, carefully trim away ¼" inside the appliqué stitches. Continue with a shape of the next size and so on, following the steps to stitch and trim.

American Beauty Rose

Refer to the block diagram and use your preferred method to appliqué the following pieces in the order listed: four 6" lengths of ¼"-wide green folded bias strips for stems, 4 A, 4 B, 1 C, 1 D, 1 E, 1 F, and 20 G.

Rose of Sharon

Refer to the block diagram and use your preferred method to appliqué the following pieces in the order listed: two 5" lengths of ¼"-wide green folded bias strips for the upper stems, two 7" lengths of ½"-wide folded bias strips for the lower stems, 13" of ½"-wide folded bias strips for the main stem, 3 D, 3 E, 3 F, 2 A, 2 I, 2 H, 1 J, and 14 G.

Whig Rose

Refer to the block diagram and use your preferred method to appliqué the following pieces in the order listed: 6 A, 6 B, 1 K, 1 C, 1 D, 1 E, 1 F, and 12 G.

Rose Tree

Refer to the block diagram and use your preferred method to appliqué the following pieces in the order listed: two 4" lengths of ½"-wide folded bias strips for the upper stems, two 6½" lengths of ½"-wide folded bias strips for the lower stems, 10" of ½"-wide folded bias strips for the main stem, 1 L, 5 D, 5 E, 5 F, and 8 G.

Wreath of Roses

Refer to the block diagram and use your preferred method to appliqué the following pieces in the order listed: four 10" lengths of ¼"-wide plaid folded bias strips for stems, 4 D, 4 E, 4 F, 4 A, 4 I, and 16 G.

Assembling the Quilt Top

1. Arrange the blocks and the quarter-square side-setting triangles in diagonal rows as shown in the assembly diagram. Do not place the corner-setting triangles yet.

Assembly diagram

2. Sew the blocks and triangles together into diagonal rows; press.

3. Pin and sew the rows together, nesting the seams.

4. Pin and sew the half-square corner-setting triangles to the quilt. Press the seams toward the triangles.

Attaching and Appliquéing the Borders

1. Referring to "Attaching Borders" on page 90 as needed, sew the 9" x 41½" pink border strips to the sides of the quilt top and the 9" x 58½" pink border strips to the top and bottom of the quilt top. Press the seams toward the borders.

2. Refer to the photo on page 32 and the quilt diagram below. Use your preferred method to appliqué the following pieces to the borders in the order listed: the remaining ½"-wide folded bias strips for the vines and stems, 8 C, 24 D, 24 E, 24 F, 24 A, 24 B, and 144 G. Note that some pieces overlap into the setting triangles.

Quilt diagram

3. Press the quilt top and carefully trim the edges to square the quilt top.

Finishing the Quilt

1. Refer to "Quiltmaking Basics" on page 88 for guidance in layering, basting, and quilting the quilt top. Leave 1" unquilted all around the perimeter of the quilt top to allow for adding the prairie points. I quilted in the ditch around each appliqué shape and added a 1½"-wide diagonal grid over the entire background of the quilt.

2. Fold each 4" plaid square in half on the diagonal; press. Fold in half on the diagonal again; press.

3. Place the quilt face down on a flat surface. Fold and pin the unquilted batting and backing to the back of the quilt. Turn the quilt face up and square up the quilt top if needed. (The excess batting and backing will be trimmed after the prairie points are added.) Unpin the batting, but leave the backing pinned to the back of the quilt.

4. Smooth the trimmed front over the batting. Evenly space and pin 18 prairie points along one side of the front of the quilt. Align the raw edge of each prairie point with the raw edge of the quilt top, tucking the corner of each prairie point into the fold of its neighbor. When you are satisfied with the spacing, stitch the prairie points to the quilt top and batting ¼" from the raw edge of the quilt top. Repeat for the three remaining sides of the quilt. Trim the edges of the batting close to the stitching line. Do not trim the backing yet.

5. Remove the pins from the backing. Trim the backing to ½" beyond the trimmed batting. Press the seam allowance toward the quilt to turn the prairie points to the outside. Fold the backing under ½" and stitch to the back side of the prairie points.

6. Refer to "Quiltmaking Basics" on page 88 to add a hanging sleeve and label.

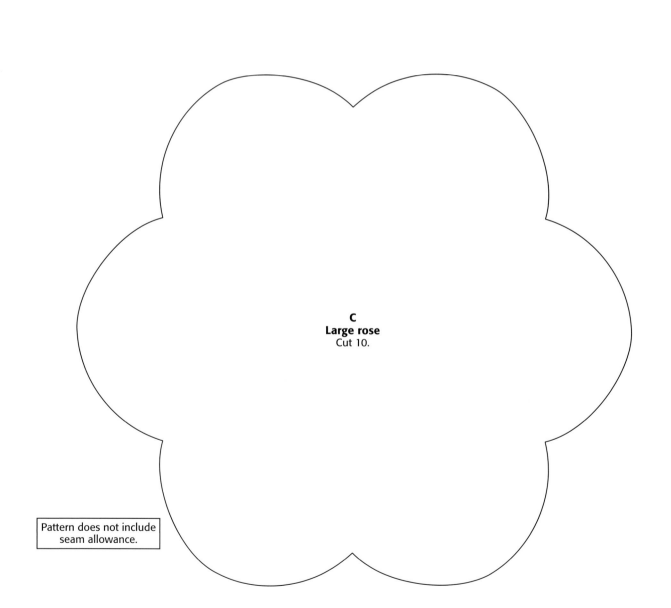

C
Large rose
Cut 10.

Pattern does not include seam allowance.

Pattern does not include
seam allowance.

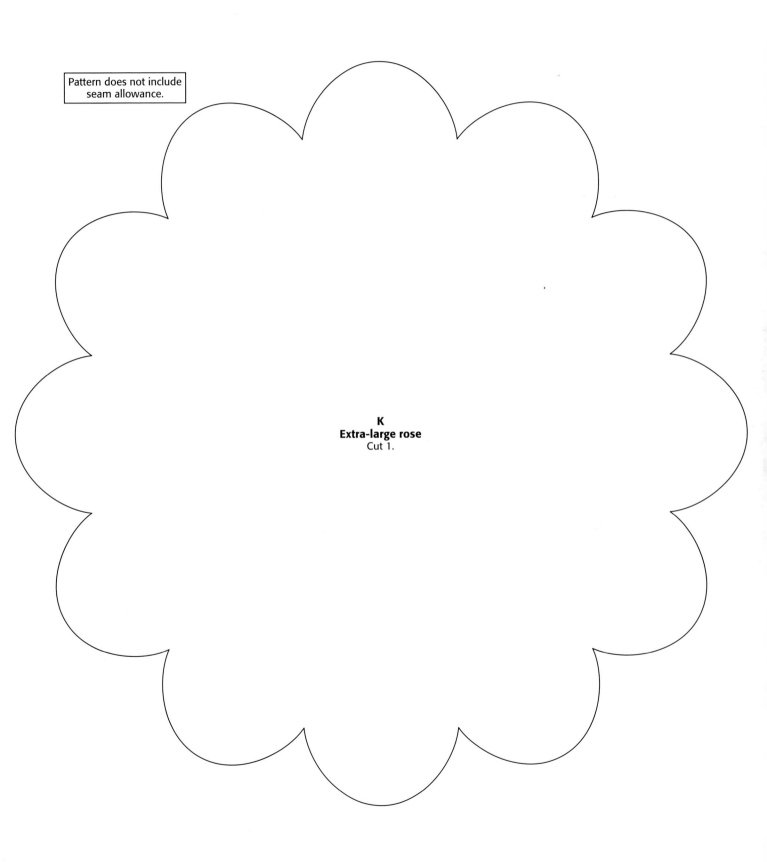

K
Extra-large rose
Cut 1.

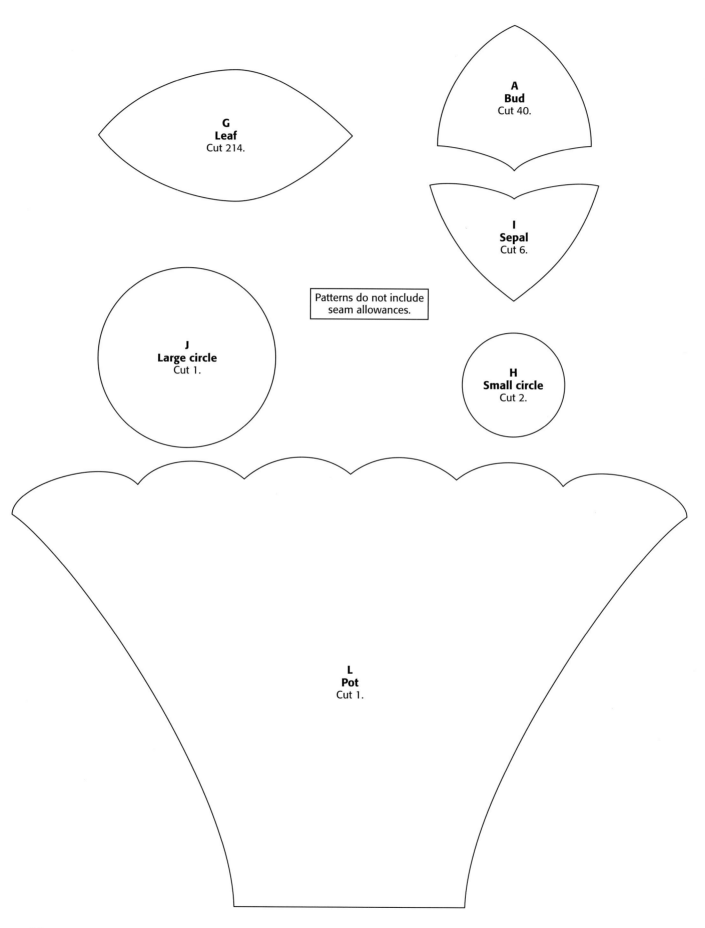

G
Leaf
Cut 214.

A
Bud
Cut 40.

I
Sepal
Cut 6.

Patterns do not include
seam allowances.

J
Large circle
Cut 1.

H
Small circle
Cut 2.

L
Pot
Cut 1.

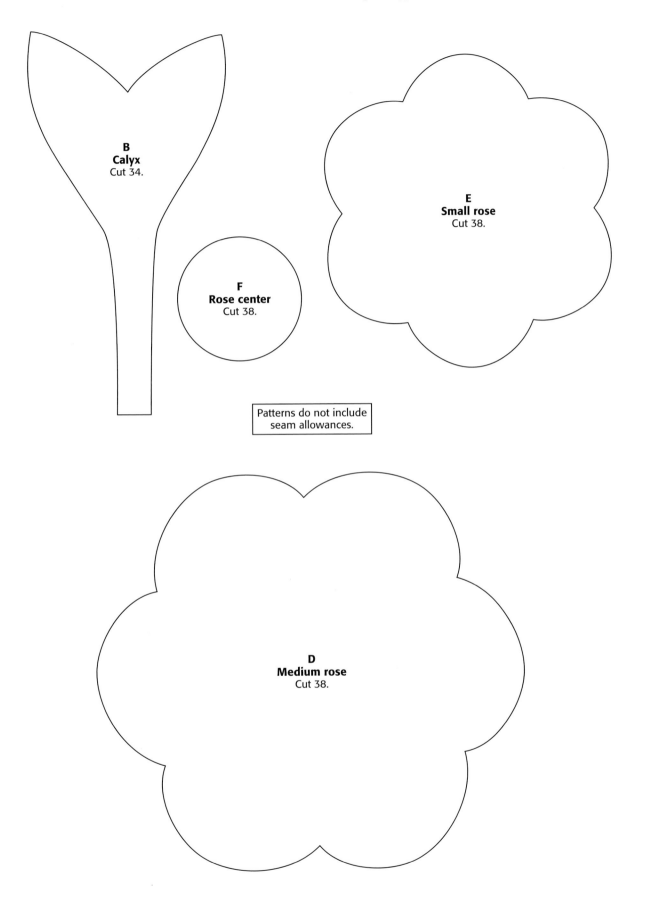

B
Calyx
Cut 34.

F
Rose center
Cut 38.

E
Small rose
Cut 38.

Patterns do not include
seam allowances.

D
Medium rose
Cut 38.

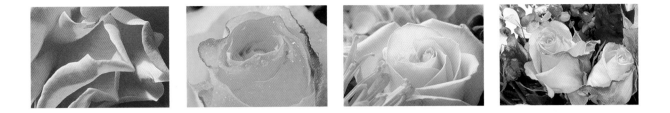

Scottish Rose
~ Throw ~

I never realized until a couple years ago that my little rose doodles actually have pedigree. Those spiral squiggles with angel-wing leaves that so entrance me are emblematic of the Glasgow style popularized by Charles Rennie Mackintosh and his fellow Scottish artisans at the turn of the twentieth century.

Transforming a squiggle into a rose that could be pieced and quilted looked to be impossible for this designer with her very literal mind-set, but then Catherine introduced me to the world of bias-tape makers and the idea became viable. There are certainly limits to the tightness of the spiral in relationship to the width of the bias strip, but with judicious urging and a hot iron to fix the curves, even Charles Rennie Mackintosh would be impressed. I used a faced appliqué method in this quilt to add dimension to the appliqué motifs. —Jennifer

Choosing Fabrics
Look for fabrics with graduated tones for the rose-spiral bias strips—minimal or tone-on-tone patterns work best for the spirals and the rose bases as well. For the checkerboards, choose blue prints with tones that vary within a narrow range, and eliminate fabrics that shout for attention.

Materials

All yardages are based on 42"-wide fabric.

- 3½ yards *total* of assorted tone-on-tone white prints for quilt center, middle border, and outer-border checkerboards
- 2⅞ yards *total* of assorted blue prints for quilt center, outer-border checkerboards, and binding
- ¾ yard *total* of assorted green prints for stems and leaf appliqués
- ⅔ yard *total* of pastel prints for rose bases
- ⅝ yard *total* of bright floral prints for rose spirals
- 4 yards of fabric for backing
- 64" x 72" piece of batting
- ¼" bias-tape maker
- Spray starch
- Cardboard tube

Cutting

All measurements include ¼" seam allowances. Cut all strips across the fabric width (selvage to selvage) unless otherwise noted. Refer to "Cutting with Templates" on page 88 for instructions on cutting appliqué shapes. The pattern for the leaf appears on page 47.

From the assorted blue prints, cut a *total* of:
- 11 strips, 3½" x 42"; crosscut into 120 squares, 3½" x 3½"
- 21 strips, 1½" x 42"; cut each strip in half widthwise to yield 42 strips, 1½" x 21"
- 7 strips, 2½" x 42"

From the assorted white prints, cut a *total* of:
- 9 strips, 3½" x 42"; crosscut into 99 squares, 3½" x 3½"
- 10 squares, 6" x 6"; cut each square twice diagonally to yield 4 quarter-square triangles (40 total)*
- 2 squares, 4" x 4"; cut each square once diagonally to yield 2 half-square triangles (4 total)*
- 5 strips, 5⅛" x 42"
- 21 strips, 1½" x 42"; cut each strip in half widthwise to yield 42 strips, 1½" x 21"

From the assorted green prints, cut a *total* of:
- ½"-wide bias strips to total approximately 160"
- 60 leaf appliqués

From the assorted pastel prints, cut a *total* of:
- 32 squares, 5" x 5"

From the assorted bright floral prints, cut:
- ½"-wide bias strips to total approximately 360"

These setting triangles are cut oversized to allow for trimming later.

Assembling the Quilt Center

1. Arrange the 3½" blue and white squares (on point) and the quarter-square side-setting triangles as shown in the assembly diagram below, taking care to distribute the patterns and tones of the blue squares for a balanced effect. Do not place the corner-setting triangles yet.
2. Sew the squares and triangles together into diagonal rows. Press the seams toward the blue squares.
3. Pin and sew the rows together, nesting the seams.
4. Pin and sew the half-square corner-setting triangles to the quilt. Press the seams toward the triangles.

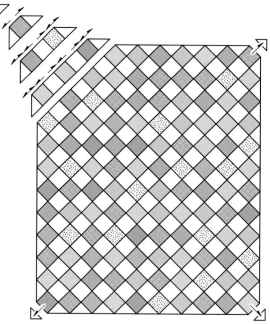

Assembly diagram

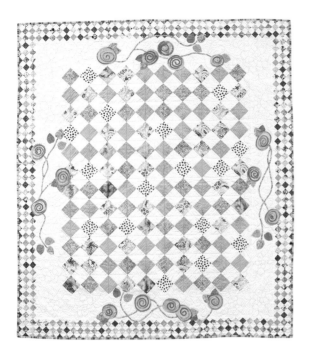

Designed by Jennifer Rounds. Pieced and appliquéd by Jennifer Rounds and Trish Katz. Machine quilted by Kathy Sandbach.

Finished Quilt: 59¾" x 66¼"

5. Square up the quilt top, trimming the edges to ¼" from the outermost corners of the blue squares.

Attaching the Borders

Refer to "Attaching Borders" on page 90 as needed.

1. Sew the 5⅛" x 42" white strips together end to end. Press the seams open. Measure the quilt through the center from side to side and cut two strips to this measurement. Pin and sew a cut strip to the top and bottom of the quilt top. Press the seams toward the borders.

2. Measure the quilt through the center from top to bottom, including the borders just added. Cut two strips to this measurement. Pin and sew a cut strip to the sides of the quilt top; press.

3. Sew three 1½"-wide blue strips and three 1½"-wide white strips together, alternating them as shown to make a strip set. Make 14 strip sets, taking care to vary the placement of the prints and tones of the blue fabrics. Press the seams in one direction. Crosscut the strips into 182 segments, 1½" wide.

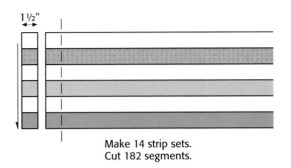

Make 14 strip sets.
Cut 182 segments.

4. Pin, nesting the seams, and sew 40 units together to make the top outer border, staggering the units as shown in the diagram below. Press carefully. Repeat to make the bottom outer border.

5. Trim ¼" from the outside of the blue squares on each short side and one long side of each unit from step 4.

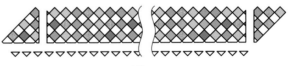

Trim.

6. Pin and sew the long trimmed edge of one unit from step 5 to the top edge of the quilt. Press the seam toward the white border. Repeat to sew the remaining unit to the bottom edge of the quilt; press.

7. Repeat step 4 with 51 units to make a side outer border. Press carefully. Make two.

8. Trim ¼" from the outside of the blue squares on one long side only.

9. Pin and sew the side borders to the quilt top, matching the points of the blue squares to the top and bottom outer-border blue squares.

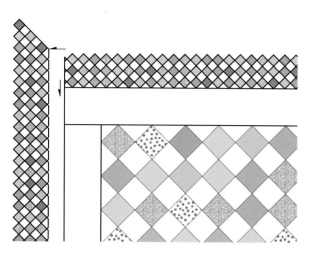

10. Stabilize the outside edge of the quilt by machine stitching with a small stitch ⅛" from the outer corners of the outermost white squares as shown. Do not trim the edges yet.

Making the Roses

1. To make a rose base, place two 5" pastel-print squares right sides together; fold into quarters.

2. Cut a quarter circle from the folded squares as shown. Don't worry about precision—the rose bases can be circular, oval, or vary in size. Diversity of shape adds to the visual interest.

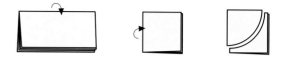

3. Unfold the squares, keeping the circles right sides together. Use a short machine stitch to sew the circles together ⅛" from the edges. Cut a small slit into one circle, taking care not to cut through to the second circle. Turn the rose base to the right side through the slit. Gently work out the curves; press.

4. Repeat steps 1–3 to make a total of 16 rose bases.

5. Refer to "Making Folded Bias Strips" on page 89 and follow the package instructions for the bias-tape maker to make ¼"-wide finished folded bias strips with the ½"-wide bright floral-print bias strips. Wrap the strips around a cardboard tube for storage.

6. Cut the bias strips into 16 lengths varying from 20" to 25".

7. Pin the end of one bias strip to your ironing board. Use the tip of a hot iron and light steam to press the strip into a coil. This is a finessing technique: pulling or twisting will distort the strip. Continue curving and pressing to the end of the strip to create a coil as shown. Lightly spray with starch and press to set the curves. Make 16 coils.

Make 16.

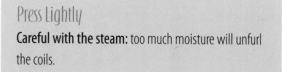

Press Lightly
Careful with the steam: too much moisture will unfurl the coils.

8. Pin a coiled strip to a rose base, keeping in mind that offset centers are just as wonderful as perfectly centered spirals. Turn under the raw end at the center of the coil and use matching thread to stitch the coil to the rose base. Continue stitching and arranging the coil so that it ends at the outer edge of the base. Some roses may be more tightly or loosely coiled than others. Tuck in the outer raw end of the coil before completing the stitching. Make 16.

Make 16.

Making the Stems and Leaves

1. Refer to "Making Folded Bias Strips" on page 89 and follow the package instructions for the bias-tape maker to make approximately 160" of ¼"-wide folded bias strips with the ½"-wide green bias strips. Wrap the strips around a cardboard tube for storage.
2. Pin two leaf shapes right sides together. Clip the curves lightly for easing as needed and use a short machine stitch to sew the leaves together ⅛" from the raw edges. Cut a small slit into one leaf, taking care not to cut through to the second leaf. Turn the leaf to the right side through the slit. Gently work out the curves and the point; press. Make 30 leaves.

Adding the Appliqués

1. Refer to the photo on page 45 to arrange and pin the roses to the white inner borders. Cut the ¼"-wide green folded bias strips into various lengths and pin them into curvy stems around and beneath the rose blossoms. Position and pin the leaves as desired.
2. Use matching thread to stitch the stems, roses, and leaves to the white borders.

Finishing the Quilt

1. Refer to "Quiltmaking Basics" on page 88 for layering, basting, and quilting the quilt top. Kathy quilted a grid through the checkerboards, and flowing stems of roses and leaves in the inner, appliquéd border.
2. Trim the edges of the quilt a generous ¼" beyond the outer corner of the outermost white squares. Use the 2½"-wide blue strips to make the binding. Baste the binding to the quilt with a ¼" seam allowance. Check to be sure that the blue corners are not cut off in the trial stitching line; adjust as needed. Sew the binding to the quilt. Finish by adding a sleeve and label.

The Mackintosh Rose

Jessie Newbery, an embroidery teacher at the Glasgow School of Art, was the source for a rose motif that Charles Rennie Mackintosh and his cohorts later developed to iconic status. The breadth and body of Mackintosh's work is impressive; not only was he an artist, he was also a craftsman and architect. He exhibited extensively at international expositions of art and design, even creating a Rose Boudoir with his wife, Margaret Macdonald, for a 1902 exhibition of modern art in Turin, Italy. The Glasgow style he popularized sits between the Arts and Crafts and Art Nouveau movements that concluded the nineteenth century and the Art Deco and Modernist styles of the early twentieth century.

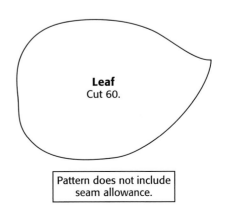

Leaf
Cut 60.

Pattern does not include
seam allowance.

Rose of Havana

~ Quilt ~

Yes, there are lots of little pieces of fabric here, but that is what happens when a quilt is inspired by a mosaic-tiled surface. I fell in love with an image of a tiled wall in a House Beautiful *article about Colonial Cuban architecture: aqua blue, tone-on-tone mosaic checkerboards framed painted images of blooming roses. Catherine, the wonderfully skilled, mathematical quilt designer (thank goodness!), rolled her eyes and said, "Let's do this as a foundation-pieced project." That was a major brainstorm: we were able to call on the very talented coterie of craftswomen in our quilt/book group to contribute roses to our "bouquet."* —Jennifer

Including Friends

There are several ways to tackle this project. The easiest is to distribute cuts of the background fabric to friends and let them choose the fabric to foundation piece the roses and rosebuds. Otherwise, get crazy and itemize and precut all the fabric pieces for the foundation piecing. No matter which option you choose, even if you decide to piece all the blocks yourself, organize the pieces according to size and use and label the stacks with sticky notes for sewing.

Materials

All yardages are based on 42"-wide fabric.

- 4¼ yards of beige print for blocks, sashing, posts, and borders
- 2⅝ yards *total* of assorted rose prints for blocks and sashing
- 1¼ yards of medium-value aqua print for sashing, posts, border, and binding
- ⅝ yard of light aqua print for sashing, posts, and border
- ½ yard *total* of assorted green prints for blocks and sashing
- 3⅝ yards of fabric for backing (vertical seam)
- 52" x 64" piece of batting
- Paper suitable for foundation piecing

Cutting

All measurements include ¼" seam allowances. Cut all strips across the fabric width (selvage to selvage).

From the rose prints, cut a *total* of:
- 12 squares, 2½" x 2½"
- 48 rectangles, 1¾" x 2½", in matching sets of 4
- 48 rectangles, 2" x 3", in matching sets of 4
- 96 rectangles, 2½" x 4", in matching sets of 4
- 48 rectangles, 3¼" x 5¼", in matching sets of 4
- 48 squares, 2⅜" x 2⅜", in matching pairs
- 31 squares, 1¾" x 1¾"
- 124 rectangles, 1½" x 1¾", in matching sets of 4

From the green prints, cut a *total* of:
- 96 rectangles, 1¼" x 2", in matching sets of 8
- 62 rectangles, 1¾" x 2½"

From the beige print, cut:
- 6 strips, 3¼" x 42"; crosscut into 96 rectangles, 2½" x 3¼"
- 3 strips, 1¼" x 42"; crosscut into 96 squares, 1¼" x 1¼"
- 5 strips, 2" x 42"; crosscut into 124 rectangles, 1½" x 2"

- 4 strips, 2½" x 42"; crosscut into 62 rectangles, 2¼" x 2½"
- 10 strips, 1¾" x 42"; crosscut into 248 rectangles, 1½" x 1¾"
- 8 strips, 2½" x 42"; crosscut into 124 squares, 2½" x 2½"
- 2 strips, 4¼" x 42"; crosscut into 62 rectangles, 1¼" x 4¼"
- 6 strips, 2" x 42"
- 10 strips, 1¼" x 42"
- 1 strip, 4¼" x 42"; crosscut into 18 rectangles, 1½" x 4¼"
- 2 strips, 9½" x 42"; crosscut into 14 rectangles, 3" x 9½"
- 4 squares, 3" x 3"

From the medium-value aqua print, cut:
- 18 strips, 1¼" x 42"
- 6 strips, 2½" x 42"

From the light aqua print, cut:
- 15 strips, 1¼" x 42"

Making the Rose Blocks

1. Make 12 copies of the rose pattern on page 56. Refer to "Foundation Piecing" on page 88 and use the 2½" rose squares, 1¾" x 2½" rose rectangles, 2" x 3" rose rectangles, 2½" x 4" rose rectangles, and 3¼" x 5¼" rose rectangles to make 12 rose units. (You will have some 2½" x 4" rectangles left over to use in the next step.) Trim each unit to 6½" square.

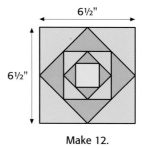

Make 12.

2. Make 48 copies of the outer rose unit pattern on page 57. Refer to "Foundation Piecing" and use the 2½" x 3¼" beige rectangles and

Designed and pieced by Catherine Comyns and Jennifer Rounds, with blocks contributed by Kim Butterworth, Valerie Chapla, and Cyndy Rymer. Machine quilted by Rachel Justus.

Finished Quilt: 47½" x 60¼"
Finished Block: 9" x 9"

the remaining 2½" x 4" rose rectangles to make 48 units in matching sets of four. Trim each unit to 2" x 5".

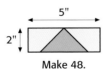

Make 48.

3. Draw a diagonal line on the wrong side of a 2⅜" rose square. Pin the marked square right sides together with a different 2⅜" rose-colored square. Sew ¼" from each side of the drawn line.

¼"

4. Cut the unit from step 3 apart on the drawn line. Press open, with the seam toward the darker fabric.

5. Repeat steps 3 and 4 to make a total of 48 units in matching sets of four.

6. Draw a diagonal line on the wrong side of each 1¼" beige square. With right sides together, pin a marked square to one end of a 1¼" x 2" green rectangle. Sew on the drawn line. Trim ¼" from the sewn line; press open with the seam toward the small triangle. Make 48 each in matching sets of eight (four and four reverse).

Make 96 total
(4 and 4 reversed in
matching sets of 8).

7. Arrange and sew a unit from step 1, four matching units each from steps 2 and 5, and eight matching units (four of each) from step 6 as shown; press. Make 12 Rose blocks.

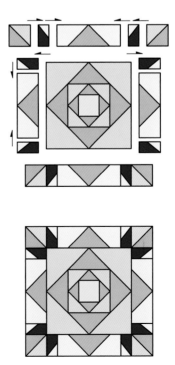

Make 12.

51

Making the Sashing Units

1. Make 31 copies of the rosebud sashing-unit pattern on page 57. Refer to "Foundation Piecing" on page 88 and use the 1¾" rose squares, 1½" x 1¾" rose rectangles, 1½" x 2" beige rectangles, and 2¼" x 2½" beige rectangles to make 31 rosebud sashing units. Trim each unit to 2" x 4¼".

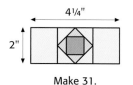

Make 31.

2. Make 62 copies of the leaf sashing-unit pattern on page 57. Refer to "Foundation Piecing" and use the 1¾" x 2½" green rectangles, 1½" x 1¾" beige rectangles, and 2½" beige squares to make 62 leaf sashing units. Trim each unit to 2" x 4¼".

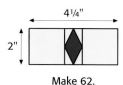

Make 62.

3. Sew a 1¼"-wide medium aqua strip between two 2"-wide beige strips to make a strip set as shown; press. Make two strip sets. Crosscut the strip sets into 62 segments, 1¼" wide.

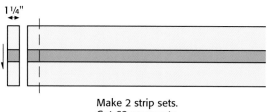

Make 2 strip sets.
Cut 62 segments.

Press for Success

To minimize distortion when sewing strips into strip sets, use a dry iron and press after sewing each seam.

4. Sew together one 1¼"-wide light aqua strip, two 1¼"-wide medium aqua strips, and two 1¼" x 42" beige strips to make a strip set as shown; press. Make two strip sets. Crosscut the strip sets into 62 segments, 1¼" wide.

Make 2 strip sets.
Cut 62 segments.

5. Arrange and sew two 1¼" x 4¼" beige rectangles, two segments each from steps 3 and 4, two leaf sashing units from step 2, and a rosebud sashing unit from step 1 as shown; press. Make 31 sashing units.

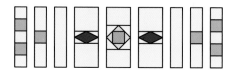

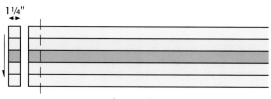

Make 31.

Making the Post Units

When making the mosaic posts, Catherine cut the 42"-long strips into two 21" lengths before sewing the strips together. If you choose to do the same, double the number of strip sets in each step.

1. Sew together a 1¼"-wide medium aqua strip, two 1¼"-wide light aqua strips, and two 1¼" x 42" beige strips to make a strip set as shown; press. Make two strip sets. Crosscut the strip sets into 40 segments, 1¼" wide.

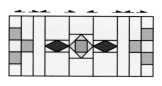

Make 2 strip sets.
Cut 40 segments.

2. Sew together three 1¼"-wide light aqua strips and two 1¼"-wide medium aqua strips to make a strip set as shown; press. Make two strip sets. Crosscut the strip sets into 40 segments, 1¼" wide.

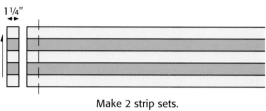

Make 2 strip sets.
Cut 40 segments.

3. Sew together three 1¼"-wide medium aqua strips and two 1¼"-wide light aqua strips to make a strip set as shown; press. Crosscut the strip set into 20 segments, 1¼" wide.

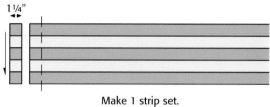

Make 1 strip set.
Cut 20 segments.

4. Arrange and sew two segments each from steps 1 and 2 along with a segment from step 3 as shown; press. Make 20 post units.

Make 20.

Making the Border Units

1. Sew together a 1¼"-wide light aqua strip, two 1¼"-wide medium aqua strips, and two 1¼"-wide beige strips to make a strip set as shown; press. Crosscut the strip set into 18 segments, 1¼" wide.

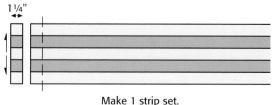

Make 1 strip set.
Cut 18 segments.

2. Sew a 1¼"-wide medium aqua strip between two 2"-wide beige strips as shown; press. Crosscut the strip set into 18 segments, 1¼" wide.

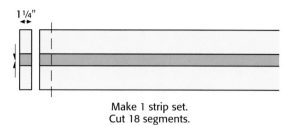

Make 1 strip set.
Cut 18 segments.

3. Arrange and sew together one segment each from steps 1 and 2 and a 1½" x 4¼" beige rectangle as shown; press. Make 18 border units.

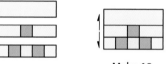

Make 18.

Assembling the Quilt Top

1. Sew together four post units and three sashing units to make a row as shown. Press the seams toward the sashing units. Make five and label them rows 1, 3, 5, 7, and 9.

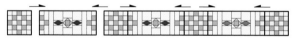
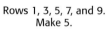

Rows 1, 3, 5, 7, and 9.
Make 5.

2. Sew together four sashing units and three blocks to make a row as shown. Press the seams toward the sashing units. Make four and label them rows 2, 4, 6, and 8.

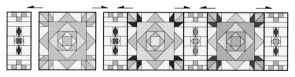

Rows 2, 4, 6, and 8.
Make 4.

3. Sew the rows from steps 1 and 2 together, alternating them as shown in the assembly diagram; press.

Assembly diagram

4. Arrange and sew four 3" x 9½" beige rectangles and five border units as shown; press. Make two and sew them to the sides of the quilt. Press the seams away from the borders.

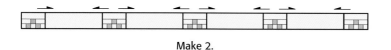

Make 2.

5. Arrange and sew three 3" x 9½" beige rectangles, four border units, and two 3" beige squares as shown; press. Make two and sew them to the top and bottom of the quilt; press.

Make 2.

Finishing the Quilt

Refer to "Quiltmaking Basics" on page 88 for guidance in layering, basting, and quilting the quilt top. Rachel quilted in the ditch to emphasize the geometry of the mosaic tiles, giving them a dimensional quality. She softened the angles of the foundation-pieced roses with curvy quilting lines and, in the beige background, created the effect of foliage with leaves and curlicues. Use the 2½"-wide medium aqua strips to bind the quilt, and finish by adding a sleeve and label.

Inspirational Spanish Tiles

Azulejos, or tiles, were the inspiration for this quilt. Using ceramic tiles for flooring and walls is very typical in Portugal, Spain, and Latin America. The tiling tradition comes from the Moorish occupation of the Iberian Peninsula, which, coincidentally, concluded in 1492, when Christopher Columbus's patrons, Ferdinand and Isabella of Spain, drove the remnants of the Moorish invaders from their lands. Moorish-influenced ceramic tiles traveled to the New World, where the grandees decorated their palaces with elaborately illustrated and brightly colored tiles.

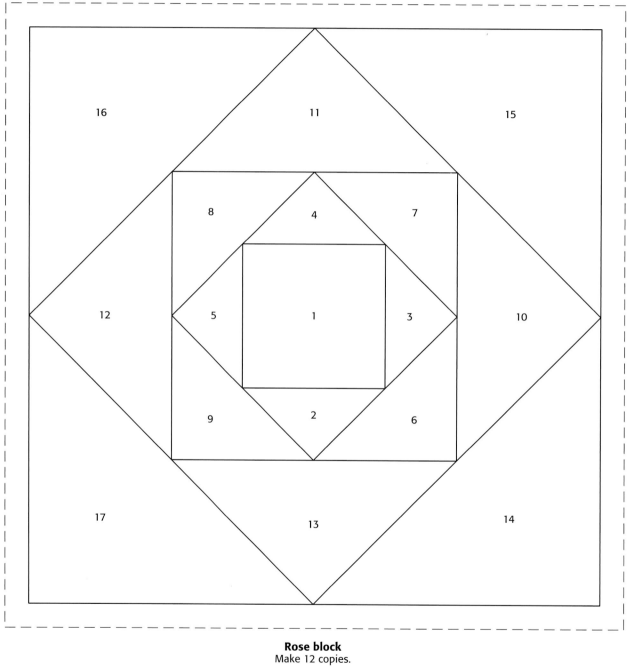

Rose block
Make 12 copies.

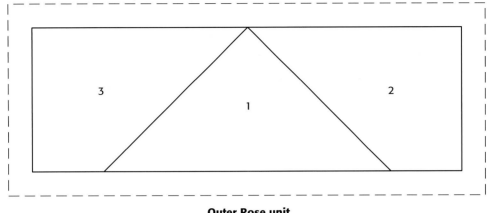

Outer Rose unit
Make 48 copies.

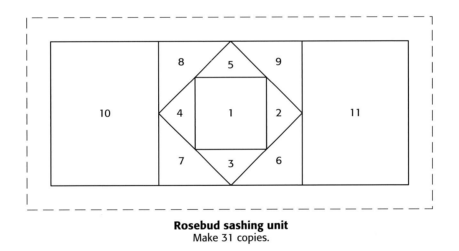

Rosebud sashing unit
Make 31 copies.

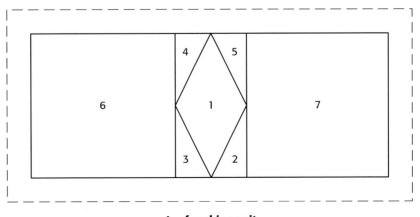

Leaf sashing unit
Make 62 copies.

Thoroughly Modern Rosie

~ Quilt ~

This pretty quilt by our friend Beate Nellemann re-creates the feeling of a trellised wall of climbing roses. Ever a clear-sighted designer, Beate took an impractical idea from an interior-design magazine and created a delightful project sure to appeal to the younger set. OK, maybe patterned beach towels are not the best source for quilting inspiration and, yes, a 1"-wide folded bias strip cannot be coaxed into a tight spiral no matter how appealing the idea. Thank goodness for Beate's clean and uncluttered Danish sensibility!

A custom bolster pillow makes a fashion-forward accent for this "Thoroughly Modern Rosie" bed quilt. The stripes of the pillows are perfect foils for the soft, rounded rose shapes— no wonder fabric designers make a habit of pairing florals and stripes.

Materials

All yardages are based on 42"-wide fabric.

- 6 yards *total* of 8 to 10 assorted light turquoise prints for blocks
- 2¾ yards *total* of assorted green prints for vines, leaves, and binding
- 1¾ yards *total* of assorted rose-colored prints for roses
- 4¾ yards of fabric for backing (vertical seam)
- 77" x 85" piece of batting
- ½" bias-tape maker
- Template material
- Green embroidery floss (optional)

Cutting

All measurements include ¼" seam allowances. Cut all strips across the fabric width (selvage to selvage) unless otherwise noted. Refer to "Cutting with Templates" on page 88 for instructions on cutting appliqué shapes. Patterns for the large and small leaf appliqués appear on page 63.

From the light turquoise prints, cut a *total* of:
- 90 squares, 8½" x 8½"

From the green prints, cut a *total* of:
- 90 bias strips, 1" x 12"
- 180 small leaf appliqués
- 90 large leaf appliqués
- 8 strips, 2½" x 42"

From the rose-colored prints, cut a *total* of:
- 36 squares, 2½" x 2½"
- 36 squares, 4" x 4"
- 36 squares, 5½" x 5½"

Appliquéing the Blocks

The patterns provided are suitable for traditional hand appliqué. Fans of fusible appliqué can reverse and adapt the patterns to suit fusible web. Beate used nylon thread to sew the bias strips to the quilt top, and a small zigzag stitch with a deeper toned green thread to lend the stems a thorny look.

1. Referring to "Making Folded Bias Strips" on page 89 and the package instructions for the bias-tape maker, make 90 folded bias strips, ½" x 12", using the 1"-wide green bias strips.
2. Pin the end of a vine to one corner of an 8½" turquoise square. Arrange and pin the vine in a curvy diagonal line across the square. Make 90.
3. Pin two small leaves to each square, tucking the ends under the vine.
4. Use your preferred method to appliqué the leaves and vine to each square. Trim the ends of the vine even with the square. Use green embroidery floss to embroider veins on each leaf, or add this detail later with quilting.

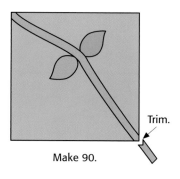

Make 90.

Assembling the Quilt Top

Refer to the photo on page 61 and the assembly diagram below. Arrange and sew the appliquéd blocks into 10 horizontal rows of nine blocks each, alternating the direction of the vines from block to block to create the effect of a rose trellis; press. Nest, pin, and sew the rows together to make the quilt top; press.

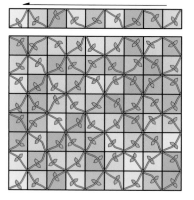

Assembly diagram

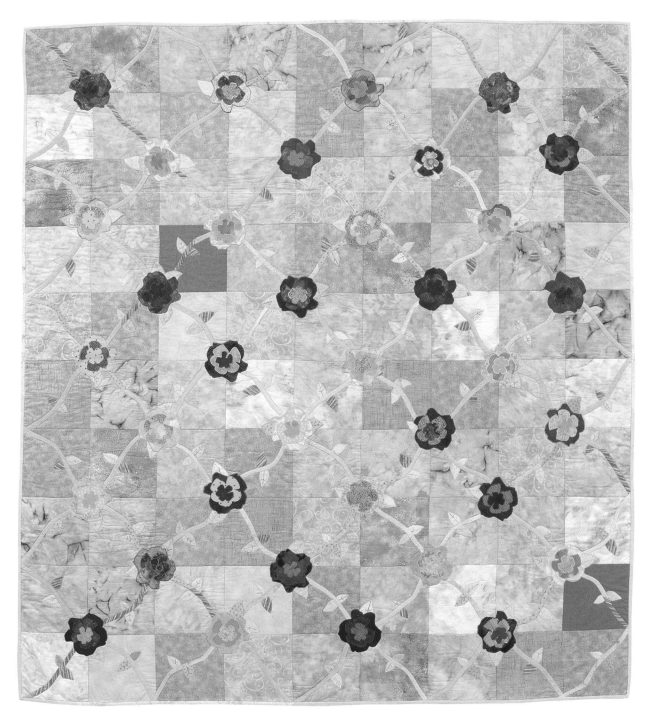

Designed and made by Beate Nellemann

Finished Quilt: 72½" x 80½" • Finished Block: 8" x 8"

Making the Roses

These free-form roses are made from three layers of fabric. Let the scissors dictate the shape of each layer.

1. Fold a 2½" rose-colored square in half as shown; press. Fold the pressed rectangle into thirds to make a cone and press again. Make 36.

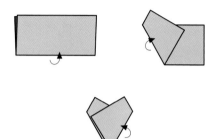

2. Working from the reverse side of the cone, cut a random curvy line along the top edge of each unit from step 1.

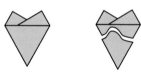

3. Repeat steps 1 and 2 using the 4" and 5½" rose-colored squares. Make 36 of each.
4. Stack and pin the trio of petals to make a rose. Make 36.

Make 36.

5. Referring to the quilt diagram below, pin a rose and two or three large leaf appliqués to the quilt top at the intersection of four blocks as shown. Use your preferred method to appliqué the leaves and roses in place.

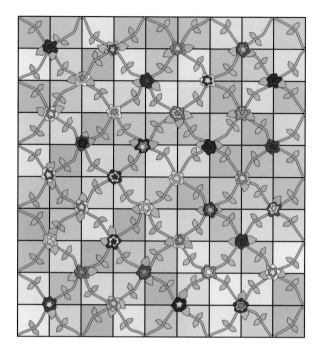

Quilt diagram

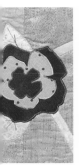

Fusing Shortcut

Beate fused the rose petal layers together and then satin stitched the edges, sometimes in higher-contrast thread. Satin-stitched edges add another decorative element to the rose motif and help emphasize the tonal variation in fabric from layer to layer.

Finishing the Quilt

Refer to "Quiltmaking Basics" on page 88 for guidance in layering, basting, and quilting the quilt top. Beate quilted in the ditch between each block and around the vines, roses, and leaves. Use the 2½"-wide green strips to bind the quilt, and finish by adding a sleeve and label.

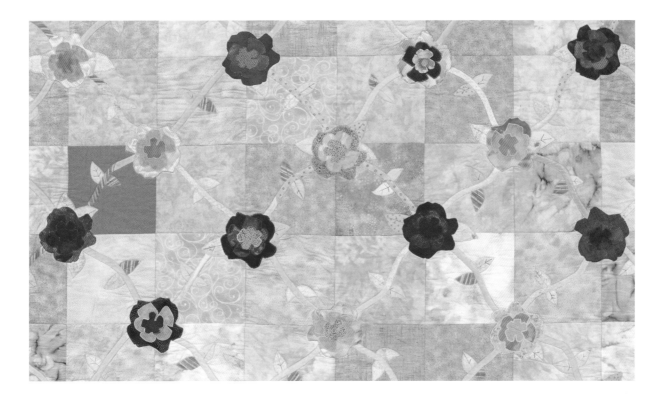

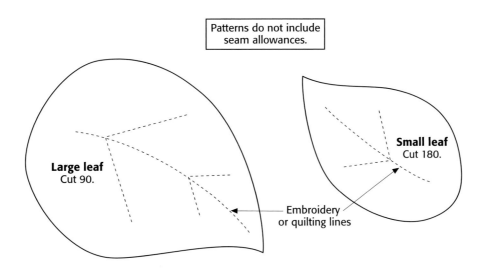

Patterns do not include seam allowances.

Large leaf
Cut 90.

Small leaf
Cut 180.

Embroidery or quilting lines

Thoroughly Modern Rosie

~ Bolster Pillow ~

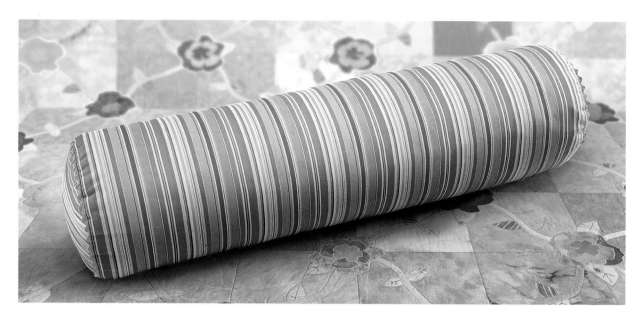

Designed and made by Jennifer Rounds

Finished Pillow: 36" length x 9" diameter (twin-size bolster)

A bolster pillow creates a great look with a bedding ensemble, especially for a fashionista who likes a dash of au courant styling. Rather than buy a pillow form and adjust to size limitations, buy 10-ounce batting on the bolt and roll it to make a pillow of an appropriate circumference and length. Compensate for the wiry texture of the heavy batting by wrapping the bolster in an additional layer of softer batting.

Even for a bolster pillow, I follow a basic square-pillow assembly formula that I have refined for home-decor sewing. In lieu of zipper closures, I overlap the edges and close with duets, trios, or quartets of buttons. I also make the pillows extra snug for a plusher look. A bolster pillow such as this one looks charming with tassels looped around accent buttons tacked to each end, although for this version, I opted instead for bolster ends trimmed in oversized rickrack.—Jennifer

Choosing Fabrics

Rather than using quilting fabric for the bolster pillow, take a look at decorator and upholstery fabrics instead. Bolster pillows need durable covers tolerant of daily wear and repeated washings. Also, decorator fabrics come in widths that accommodate longer bolsters without piecing. I was delighted to find a striped denim-weight cotton that was a perfect match for Beate's quilt. After that, I just had to make a coordinating striped silk pillow too (see page 75).

Materials

All yardages are based on 42"-wide fabric unless otherwise noted.

- ▸ 1 yard of 10-ounce batting on the bolt (45" wide)
- ▸ 1 package of crib-size batting (cotton or polyester)
- ▸ 1½ yards of fabric for bolster cover
- ▸ 2 yards of oversized rickrack (½" or wider)
- ▸ Marking pencil
- ▸ 4 decorative buttons, 1" diameter

Cutting

All measurements include ¼" seam allowances.

From the bolster fabric, cut:
- ▸ 2 circles, 9½" in diameter
- ▸ 1 rectangle, 36" x 36½"

From the rickrack, cut:
- ▸ 2 pieces, 36" long

Assembling the Bolster

1. Unfold the 10-ounce batting and place it on a clean, flat surface. Trim the batting width to 36" and save the scraps. Starting at one end, roll the batting into a tube. Make sure the tube is reasonably even and tight. Use a long running stitch to sew the end of the batting to the roll.

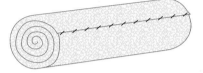

2. Unroll the crib batting, trim the width to 36", and save the scraps. Place the rolled batting from step 1 at one end and roll it up in the trimmed crib batting. Add layers of batting until the bolster measures 30" in circumference. Use a long running stitch to sew the end of the batting to the roll.

3. Cut two circles, 9½" in diameter, from the 10-ounce batting scraps. Use long running stitches to sew a circle to one end of the bolster. Before taking the last stitches, fill in the space between the end of the bolster and the batting circle with the scraps from both trimmed battings. Repeat with the second batting circle and remaining scraps at the other end of the bolster.

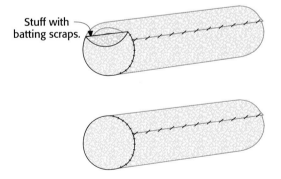

Stuff with batting scraps.

Making the Bolster Cover

1. Spread the 36" x 36½" rectangle of bolster fabric right side down on a clean, flat surface and place the bolster at one end, across the fabric width. Roll up the bolster in the fabric and place a pin where the ends overlap.

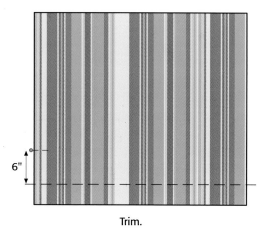

2. Unroll the fabric and trim it to 6" beyond the point pin-marked in step 1.

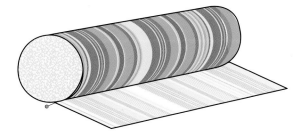

Trim.

3. Fold one side edge of the bolster fabric ¼" to the wrong side; press. Fold again, ½" this time, and press. Pin and sew the hem a scant ⅛" from the pressed fold and then again, ⅛" from the finished edge; press.

4. Repeat step 3 at the other side edge of the fabric rectangle, this time making the second fold to measure 1½". Pin and sew the hem

a scant ⅛" from the pressed fold and then again, ⅛" from the finished edge; press. This will be the finished edge for the buttonholes.

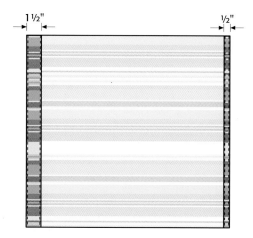

5. Working from one edge of the bolster cover, mark 1"-wide buttonholes, spacing them evenly across the width of the bolster cover. Make the buttonholes and cut them open.

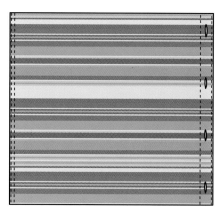

6. Once again, roll the bolster in the fabric cover. Pin the overlap at each end and carefully remove the bolster from the cover. Baste the overlaps as shown.

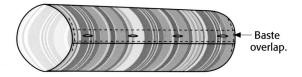

Baste overlap.

7. Pin one 36"-long piece of rickrack around one end of the bolster cover with the cut ends facing outward as shown; baste. Repeat with the second length of rickrack at the other end.

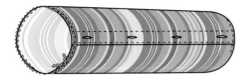

8. Fold one 9½" fabric circle into quarters and press. These pressed folds will serve as markers for pinning the bolster cover ends to the cover. Repeat, using the second 9½" fabric circle.

9. Fold the bolster cover in half lengthwise so the buttonhole edge is centered between the two folds as shown. Pin-mark the folds. Match the pins and fold the cover again; pin-mark.

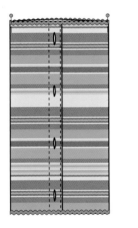 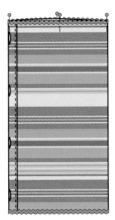

10. Turn the bolster cover to the wrong side and with right sides together, match the pins to the pressed folds in one fabric circle. Pin carefully around the perimeter, making sure to ease the fit of the circle to the bolster cover. Repeat, matching, pinning, and easing the remaining fabric circle at the other end of the bolster cover.

11. Sew each circle to the bolster cover with a ¼" seam. Turn the cover right side out; press lightly. Topstitch the rickrack to the bolster cover; this will help the exposed edge of the rickrack stand up from the end of the bolster.

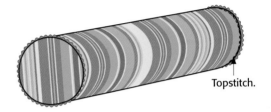

Topstitch.

12. Insert the bolster form into its cover, adding additional layers of batting if the cover is too loose. When you are satisfied with the fit, pin the buttonhole edge closed. Mark for button placement, remove the bolster pillow, and sew the buttons in place. Reinsert the bolster pillow and fasten the buttons in the bolster cover.

Bed of Roses

～ Baby Quilt ～

As a mother of two beautiful young women, I remember their newborn days with nostalgic tenderness. I hoped their futures would be as sweet as a bed of roses. If not the most practical of wishes, perhaps a symbolic gesture such as this quilted bed of roses can serve as a memento of a mother's dreams.

This is a great project for quilting pen pals or for quilt-shop hoppers. Take along a plastic template the size of the finished hexagon and use it to audition roses and estimate the rose yield in a width of fabric before making a purchase. For a lush garden, select roses that range in diameter from 1½" to 3". The challenge is to resist piecing the top until the rose collection is complete. This hands-off tactic assures a better distribution of rose colors and textures across the quilt's surface.

Finally, be very careful if you use a rotary cutter to cut the hexagons and triangles for this quilt. I succumbed to the lure of fast-and-easy cutting, but I used an 18mm rotary cutter and a 6"x 8"cutting mat that I could rotate as I cut. Keep your eyes on the blade and your fingertips at all times!—Catherine

Materials

All yardages are based on 42"-wide fabric unless otherwise noted.

- 3⅛ yards of pink print for background
- 2½ yards *total* of assorted green prints for triangles, leaf appliqués, and bias binding
- 1¾ yards *total* of assorted rose-motif prints*
- Scraps of 3 pink prints for rose appliqués
- 3¼ yards of fabric for backing
- 54" x 60" piece of batting
- See-through template material or 1½" I Spy Quilt Template by Ardco**
- Fine-point marking pen
- Freezer paper

*This is an estimate. Exact yardage will depend upon the size of the roses and the number of re-peats in the fabrics you choose.

**See "Resources" on page 94.

Cutting

All measurements include ¼" seam allowances. Cut all strips across the fabric width (selvage to selvage) unless otherwise noted. Refer to "Cutting with Templates" on page 88 for instructions on cutting appliqué shapes. Patterns appear on page 74 for the hexagon and triangle, the leaf, the outer and center rose petals, and the rose spiral appliqués.

From the assorted rose-motif prints, cut a *total* of:
- 149 hexagons*

From the assorted green prints, cut a *total* of:
- 344 triangles
- 2 leaf appliqués
- 2½"-wide bias strips to measure 288"

From the pink print, cut:
- 2 lengths, 40" x 50"

From the pink scraps, cut a *total* of:
- 1 outer rose petal appliqué
- 1 center rose petal appliqué
- 1 rose spiral

*Center the template on a rose motif, trace around the template, and then cut carefully on the drawn line.

Piecing the Bed of Roses

1. Finger-press each hexagon in half, right sides together. Finger-press 298 green triangles in half, wrong sides together. Unfold the pieces.

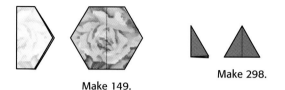

Make 149.　　　　　　Make 298.

2. Place a hexagon on a triangle, right sides together and matching the finger-pressed creases, and sew. Repeat for the opposite side of the hexagon. Press the seams toward the hexagon. Make 149.

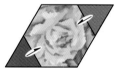

Make 149.

3. Sew eight units from step 2 together, matching the seams; press. Make two rows.

Make 2.

4. Add 10 triangles to each row from step 3 as shown. Press and label these rows 1 and 15.

Rows 1 and 15.
Make 2.

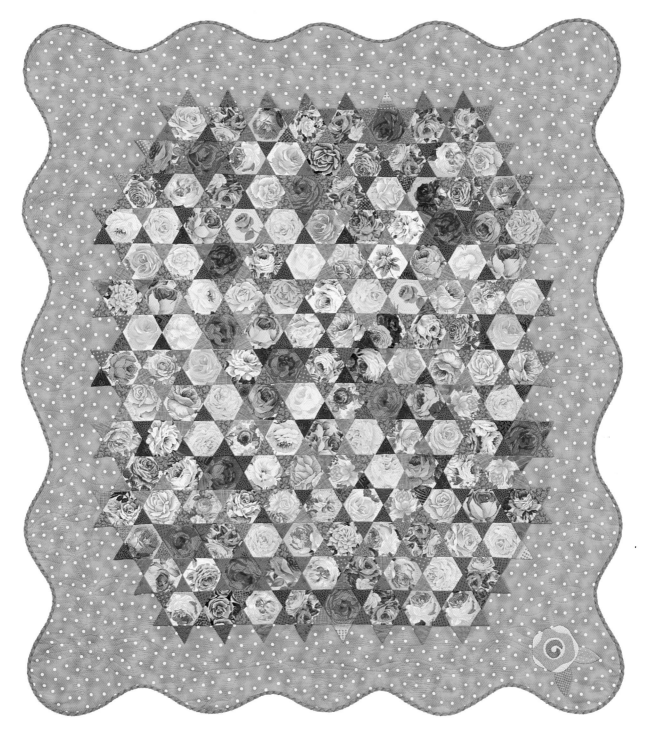

Designed and made by Catherine Comyns, with generous assistance from Trish Katz

Finished Quilt: 45½" x 50" (approximate)

5. Sew nine units from step 2 together as shown; press. Add a triangle to each end; press. Make two rows and label these rows 2 and 14.

Rows 2 and 14.
Make 2.

6. Sew 10 units from step 2 together as shown; press. Add a triangle to each end; press. Make six rows and label these rows 3, 5, 7, 9, 11, and 13.

Rows 3, 5, 7, 9, 11, and 13.
Make 6.

7. Sew 11 units from step 2 together as shown; press. Add a triangle to each end; press. Make five rows and label these rows 4, 6, 8, 10, and 12.

Rows 4, 6, 8, 10, and 12.
Make 5.

8. Refer to the assembly diagram below to arrange rows 1 through 15, staggering them and aligning the base of a rose in one row to a triangle in the next row. Pin carefully and sew the rows together; press.

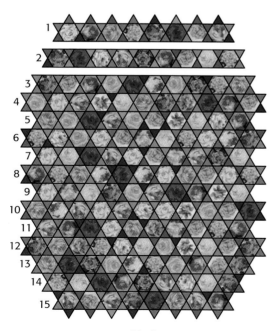

Assembly diagram

Attaching the Quilt Center to the Background

1. Piece together the two 40" x 50" pieces of background fabric. Press the seams open and trim to measure 50" x 56".
2. Fold the pieced background vertically and horizontally to find its center point; press lightly. Using the creases as a guide, center, pin, and baste the pieced quilt center to the background fabric.
3. Use matching thread to appliqué the quilt center to the background fabric. If desired, trim away the background fabric ½" inside the appliqué stitches.
4. Refer to the photo on page 71. Pin the outer rose petal to the lower-right corner of the quilt top. Tuck the leaves under the outer rose petal and stitch the leaves in place. Stitch the outer rose petal in place, and then layer and stitch the center rose petals and the spiral to the outer rose petal.

Finishing the Quilt

1. Refer to "Quiltmaking Basics" on page 88 for guidance in layering, basting, and quilting the center area of the quilt top. I quilted a 2¼"-diameter circle in each hexagon and then quilted in the ditch around the outer triangle "leaves."
2. Draw a line on each side of the quilt, 6" from the outer points of the appliquéd leaves.
3. Cut a 56"-long piece of freezer paper. Fold the paper widthwise into quarters. Cut a gentle scallop along one edge of the folded paper as shown.

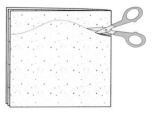

4. Unfold the paper and press it to one side of the quilt, using the line you drew in step 2 as a guide for positioning the inside curve of the scalloped edge. Trace the scallop along the edge of the quilt. Remove the freezer-paper template and repeat to mark the opposite side.

5. Repeat steps 3 and 4 to mark the top and bottom of the quilt, using a piece of freezer paper 50" long. Round the scallops at the corners as shown.

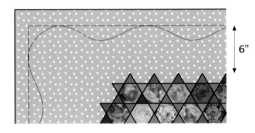

6. Machine baste directly on the scalloped lines, and then quilt the border, staying within the scalloped area. I quilted a leafy vine to echo the scalloped edge, and quilted roses in the corners.

7. Stay stitch along the basted line you stitched in step 6. Trim the quilt ⅛" outside the stay-stitched line.

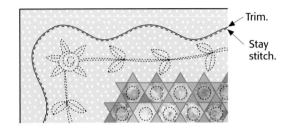

8. Referring again to "Quiltmaking Basics" on page 88, use the 2½"-wide green bias strips to bind the quilt, and finish by adding a sleeve and label.

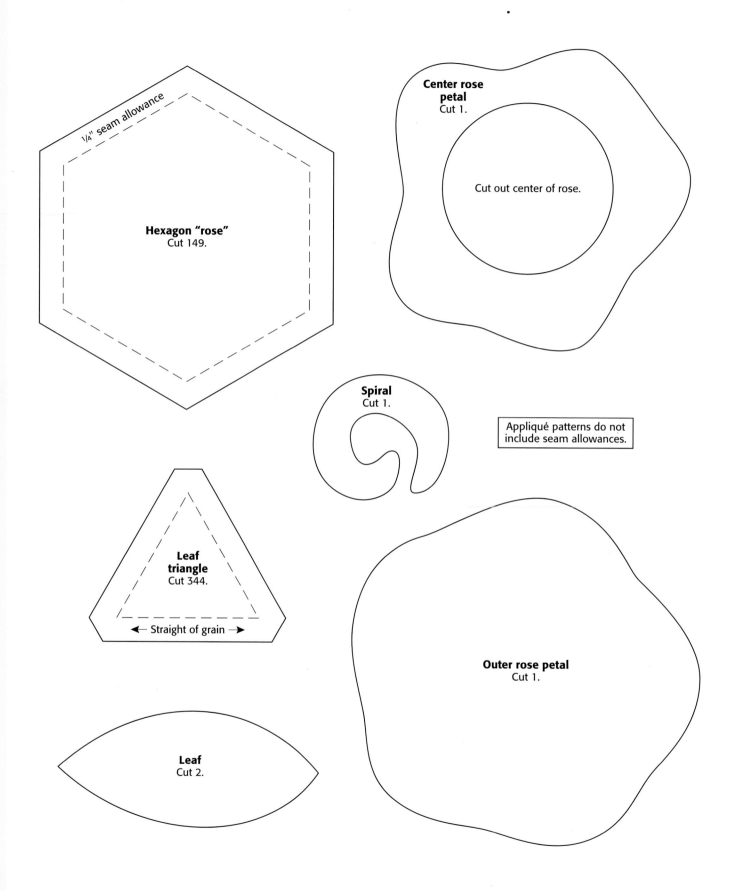

¼" seam allowance

Hexagon "rose"
Cut 149.

Center rose petal
Cut 1.

Cut out center of rose.

Spiral
Cut 1.

Applíqué patterns do not include seam allowances.

Leaf triangle
Cut 344.

← Straight of grain →

Outer rose petal
Cut 1.

Leaf
Cut 2.

Rose and
Ribbon Strips

~ Pillow ~

Designed and made by Jennifer Rounds

Finished Pillow: 16" x 16"

Quiltmaking skills and tools like cutting mats, rotary cutters, and rulers can revolutionize making projects for the home. With sharp skills in strip piecing, pattern matching, and creating mitered edges, anyone can become a home-decor guru. This is a basic pillow cover that employs quiltmaking essentials; however, with the addition of couture elements like silk and luscious trims, this simple pillow becomes a chic decorative accent.

This project is for an unrepentant dupioni silk addict, especially for one who loves the iridescent weaves that shimmer with color change. Rose-themed trims are particularly easy to find, but look for quality goods with broader color choice and more interesting designs. Warning! Half-yard cuts of trim and luxury fabrics cast a lure like fat quarters: they are way too easy to buy.

Once I perfect a pillow design, I spin embellished and unembellished variations until I run out of fabric and trims. Every quilt deserves an accent pillow; I let the quilt tell me what it wants.—Jennifer

Materials

All yardages are based on 42"-wide fabric.

- ▸ 1⅜ yards *total* of assorted rose-colored dupioni silks for pillow and pillow back
- ▸ ⅝ yard of cotton fabric for foundation
- ▸ 3½ yards *total* of laces, ribbons, and trims
- ▸ 2 decorative buttons, 1" diameter
- ▸ 1 pillow form, 16" x 16"*
- ▸ Marking pencil
- ▸ Beads, buttons, and silk roses (optional)

*This is a tight fit. Choose a high-quality form, which will be more malleable and easier to mold.

Cutting

All measurements include ¼" seam allowances. Cut all strips across the fabric width (selvage to selvage).

From the assorted rose-colored dupioni silks, cut a *total* of:

- ▸ 10 to 15 strips, 20" long, in widths varying from 1½" to 3"
- ▸ 2 rectangles, 14½" x 17½"

From the cotton fabric, cut:

- ▸ 1 square, 17½" x 17½"

From the assorted trims, cut a *total* of:

- ▸ 6 to 8 strips, 18" long

Making the Pillow Front

The trims in the featured pillow were added after the strips were sewn to the foundation as described in "Embellishing the Pillow Front" at right. Adjust the following steps to add any trims and laces designed to be sewn into seams.

1. Arrange the assorted rose silk strips in a pleasing sequence of widths and tones. Number the sequence or live dangerously and sew the strips spontaneously.
2. Pin the first silk strip right side up to the top edge of the 17½" foundation square. Baste the outer edge of the strip to the foundation.

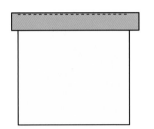

3. Pin the second strip, right sides together, to the free edge of the first strip and the foundation. Sew the strips together (and to the foundation) with a ¼" seam. Flip the second strip open and press the seam.

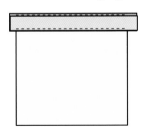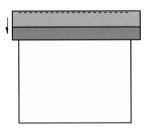

4. Repeat the process of pinning, sewing, flipping, and pressing with each strip until the foundation is completely covered. Turn the pillow front to the wrong side and stay stitch a generous ⅛" around the perimeter of the foundation. Trim the overhanging ends of the silk strips; press.

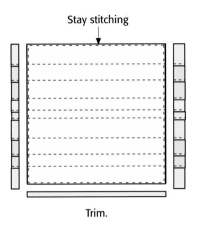

Stay stitching

Trim.

Embellishing the Pillow Front

1. Place the pillow front right side up on a clean, flat surface and arrange the 18" lengths of trim on the pillow front as desired.
2. Pin and sew each trim to the pillow front by hand or machine. If the trim is bulky, place it on the pillow front so that the bulky elements don't get caught in the seam. Some can simply be folded away from the seam. This prevents mangling the ends of the trims.

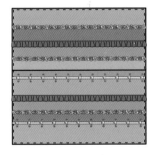

3. Embellish with beads, buttons, and silk roses as desired.

Making the Pillow Back

1. Fold ¼" to the wrong side along one 17½" edge of a silk backing rectangle; press. Fold the hemmed edge under ¼" again; press and pin. Topstitch along the folded edge and along the first fold.

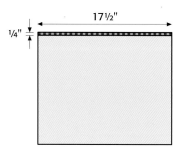

17½"

¼"

2. Fold ¼" to the wrong side along one 17½" edge of the remaining backing rectangle; press. Fold the hemmed edge under again, this time 1½"; press and pin. Topstitch along the folded edge and along the first fold.
3. Mark 1" buttonholes 5½" from each side edge of the unit from step 2. Make the buttonholes.

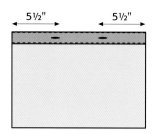

5½"   5½"

Assembling the Pillow

1. Place the pillow front right side up on a clean, flat surface. Mark the top edge if necessary.
2. Place the backing unit with buttonholes and then the second backing unit wrong side up over the pillow front, aligning the raw edges as shown. (The units will overlap at the

center.) Check the ends of the trims to make sure the ¼" seam line will accommodate any bulk.

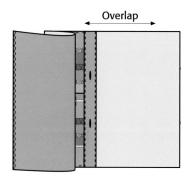

Overlap

3. Use a ¼" seam to sew around the perimeter of the pillow. An overlock stitch minimizes fraying.
4. Turn the pillow right side out. Open the buttonholes. Insert the pillow form.

Finessing the Pillow Form

Be careful inserting the pillow form into the cover; it is a tight fit. Slide the pillow under the buttonhole edge first and then push the form up so the inside piece can ease over the bulk of the pillow. This will be a strain, but work it in slowly and carefully. Once the form is fully covered, adjust it to fill the corners.

5. Make sure both the inside piece and the top piece with the buttonholes are aligned and smooth. Pin and then mark the button placement. Remove the pillow form to sew the buttons. Reinsert the pillow form when finished and button the pillow cover.

Bonus "Rose Petal"
Pillow

Nothing could be easier than this quick pillow cover. Buy ½ yard (be sure it is a full 18") of luxury fabric. This one is a silk chiffon with torn petals sewn down in rows—easy enough to reproduce by sewing parallel rows of torn chiffon "petals" to an unembellished fabric. Make sure the crosswise fabric edges are straight; trim as necessary to achieve 18". Fold the fabric into thirds, right sides together, overlapping the selvage edges until the fabric measures 18" x 18". Sew both sides of the pillow cover with ¼" seams. Turn the cover right side out and insert an 18" pillow form.

Garden Party

— Quilt —

The rose construction technique for "Garden Party" came from a project Jean Wells made for her daughter Valori's book Stitch 'n Flip Quilts (see "Resources" on page 94). I immediately whipped together a bouquet of roses when I began dreaming up ideas for A Dozen Roses, but then the pieced flowers languished for months as sad reminders of a stillborn idea. (Jean did not back herself into a design nightmare as I did when I trimmed the roses into squares.)

I remained stymied until I needed to come up with a project idea for a New York Beauties class I would be taking from Jean at an Empty Spools seminar in Pacific Grove, California. Desperation sparked my creativity and, all of a sudden, I saw my angular roses softening their pointy edges and rediscovering their bountiful, curvy nature. Why not make New York Beauty roses?

Some creative gestations are painfully slow, but I am so pleased that Jean and Catherine, my table partner at Asilomar, were midwives for the birth of this quilt. Jean was the first quilter I interviewed for The Quilter magazine back in 1999, and I think it is apt that she is a part of the creative trail I have traveled in making this book. Kudos to Valori too, as she was also a partner in absentia to this creative escapade.—Jennifer

Materials

All yardages are based on 42"-wide fabric.

- 7⅝ yards *total* of assorted blue and aqua prints in a wide range of values for pieced arcs, block backgrounds, 16-patch units, inner border, outer border, and binding
- 2½ yards *total* of assorted rose-colored prints for rose units and middle border*
- 1¼ yards *total* of assorted green prints in a wide range of values for pieced arcs
- ⅛ yard *total* of assorted yellow prints for rose units
- 4¼ yards of fabric for backing
- 68" x 76" piece of batting
- Freezer paper
- Paper suitable for foundation piecing

*This yardage is a "generous" approximate. Exact yardage will vary depending upon the size and number of strips used for each rose unit.

Cutting

All measurements include ¼" seam allowances. Cut all strips across the fabric width (selvage to selvage).

From the assorted rose-colored prints, cut a *total* of:
- 6 strips, 1½" x 42"
- Approximately 100 strips varying in size from 1" x 20" to 3" x 20"*

From the assorted blue and aqua prints, cut a *total* of:
- 265 squares, 2½" x 2½"
- 60 squares, 4" x 4"
- 20 squares, 7" x 7"
- 84 squares, 4½" x 4½"
- 12 squares, 8½" x 8½"
- 4 squares, 16½" x 16½"
- 12 strips, 2½" x 42"; cut each strip in half widthwise to yield 24 strips, 2½" x 21"
- 8 strips, 2½" x 42"

*You may wish to cut half the strips now and the rest as you complete the rose units.

From the assorted green prints, cut a *total* of:
- 80 rectangles, 2" x 2½"
- 48 rectangles, 2½" x 4"
- 16 rectangles, 4" x 7"

From the freezer paper, cut:**
- 5 circles, 4" in diameter
- 3 circles, 8" in diameter
- 1 circle, 16" in diameter

**To make a stiffer circle template, layer and press together several sheets of freezer paper.

Making the Roses

The roses are built in log-cabin fashion around an odd-shaped center. Scrap strips are perfect starters, especially for the small roses, but the large rose will eat up strip length quickly. Use narrower strip widths for the small roses and increase the widths for the larger ones. Vary the value of the fabrics spiral by spiral to create the look of unfurling petals. Try light to dark or dark to light value progressions or play with two-tone combinations, such as a pretty peach-and-pink duet or a pulsing pairing of magenta and orange.

1. Cut out an odd-shaped piece of yellow print no more than 1½" across. A five- to six-sided shape works best.
2. Place a random rose-colored strip along one edge of the yellow piece, right sides together; sew.
3. Flip open the rose-colored strip and finger-press the seam toward the strip.
4. Place another rose-colored strip on the next side of the unit from step 3; sew and finger-press.

Designed and pieced by Jennifer Rounds.
Machine quilted by Kathy Sandbach.

Finished Quilt: 64½" x 72½"

5. Continue sewing, flipping, and finger-pressing until the circuit around the yellow center is complete. Trim excess fabric from the back as needed; press.

Enhancing Your Roses

For an enhanced dimensional effect, sew thin yellow-toned strips together to create fabric for the rose centers. Also, don't worry about centering the rose center within its petals. The rose can be built asymmetrically or, later on, can be cut asymmetrically using the circle template.

6. Continue adding circuits of strips to build the rose until it is approximately 1" larger than the 4" freezer-paper circle template. Use wider strips for the last circuit to avoid thick seams at the edges of the unit. Press.

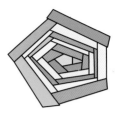

7. Press a 4" freezer-paper circle template shiny side down to the wrong side of the rose unit from step 6. Trim the rose to approximately ½" larger than the freezer paper.

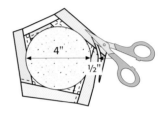

8. Turn the seam allowance over the edge of the freezer paper; baste.

9. Repeat steps 1–8 to make a total of five rose units using the 4" circle templates, three rose units using the 8" circle templates, and one rose unit using the 16" circle template.

Making the Foundation-Pieced Arcs

1. Make 20 copies of the small arc pattern on page 87. Refer to "Foundation Piecing" on page 88 and use the 2½" blue and aqua squares and the 2" x 2½" green rectangles to make 20 small arc units. Sew four arcs together as shown; press. Make five.

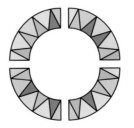 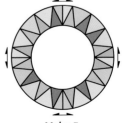

Make 5.

2. Make 12 copies of the medium arc pattern on page 87. Refer to "Foundation Piecing" and use the 4" blue and aqua squares and the 2½" x 4" green rectangles to make 12 medium arc units. Sew four arcs together; press. Make three.

3. Make four copies of the large arc pattern on page 86. Refer to "Foundation Piecing" and use the 7" blue and aqua squares and the 4" x 7" green rectangles to make four large arc units. Sew the arcs together; press.

Making the Rose Blocks

1. Center and carefully pin a 4" rose onto a small arc unit. Appliqué the rose to the foundation-pieced unit. Repeat with the remaining small, medium, and large roses and their corresponding arc units. Carefully remove the foundation paper and freezer paper.

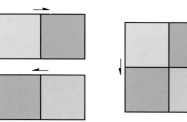

2. Arrange and sew four 4½" blue and aqua squares to make a four-patch unit as shown; press. Make five.

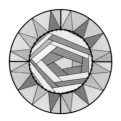

Make 5.

3. Repeat step 2 using the 8½" blue and aqua squares. Make three.

4. Repeat step 2 using the 16½" blue and aqua squares. Make one.

5. Center and pin a small rose to a unit from step 2. Use your preferred method to appliqué the rose to the four-patch unit;

press. If desired, trim away the excess fabric from behind the rose. Make five.

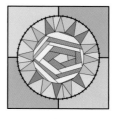

Make 5.

6. Repeat step 5 using the medium roses and the units from step 3. Make three.

7. Repeat step 5 using the large rose and the unit from step 4. Make one.

Making the 16-Patch Units

1. Sew together four 2½"-wide assorted blue and aqua strips to make a scrappy strip set as shown; press. Make six strip sets. Crosscut the strip sets into 36 segments, 2½" wide.

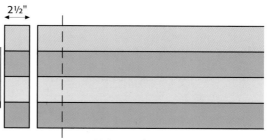

2½"

Make 6 strip sets.
Cut 36 segments.

Note: To control color and value flow as seen on page 80, consider cutting and sewing squares instead of strips.

2. Alternating the direction of the seams, nest, pin, and sew four segments from step 1 together to make a 16-patch unit. Make nine.

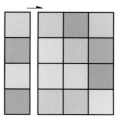

16-patch block.
Make 9.

Assembling the Quilt Top

Arrange the small, medium, and large rose blocks and the 16-patch units in sections as shown in the assembly diagram. Working one section at a time, sew the blocks and units into rows, and then the rows into sections, pressing the seams in alternating directions whenever possible. Sew the sections together; press.

Assembly diagram

Making and Attaching the Inner Border

Refer to the quilt diagram at right for guidance as needed when adding all borders.

1. Sew together twenty-eight 2½" blue and aqua squares to make an inner-border strip; press. Make three. Sew one border to the left edge of the quilt top. Press the seams toward the border. Nest the seams, pin, and sew the two remaining strips together. Sew them to the right edge of the quilt top; press.
2. Sew together twenty-seven 2½" blue and aqua squares to make an inner-border strip; press. Make three. Sew one border to the top of the quilt top; press. Nest the seams, pin, and sew the two remaining strips together. Sew this border to the bottom of the quilt top; press.

Attaching the Middle Borders

Refer to "Attaching Borders" on page 90 for guidance as needed.

1. Sew the 1½" x 42" rose strips together end to end. Press the seams open. Measure the quilt from top to bottom and cut two 1½"-wide strips to this measurement. Sew a trimmed strip to the left and right edges of the quilt top. Press the seams toward the newly added borders.
2. Measure the quilt top through the center from side to side including the borders just added. Cut two 1½"-wide strips to this measurement and sew them to the top and bottom of the quilt top; press.

Making and Attaching the Outer Border

Sew together sixteen 4½" blue and aqua squares to make an outer-border strip; press. Make four. Sew a strip to the left and right edges of the quilt top. Press the seams away from the newly added borders. Sew the remaining strips to the top and bottom; press.

Quilt diagram

Finishing the Quilt

Refer to "Quiltmaking Basics" on page 88 for guidance in layering, basting, and quilting the quilt top. Kathy machine quilted an overall design of leaves and blossoms. Use the 2½"-wide blue and aqua strips to bind the quilt, and finish by adding a sleeve and label.

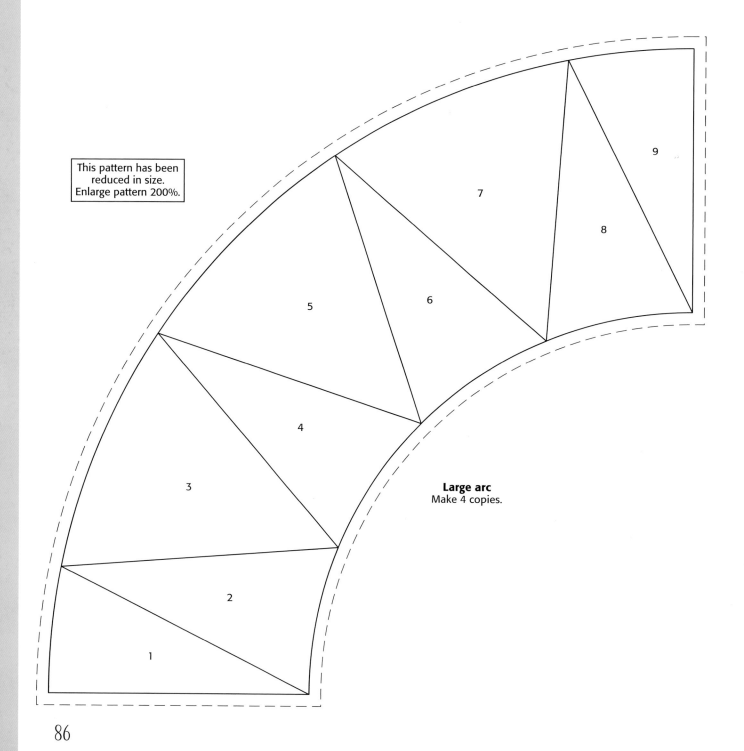

This pattern has been reduced in size.
Enlarge pattern 200%.

Large arc
Make 4 copies.

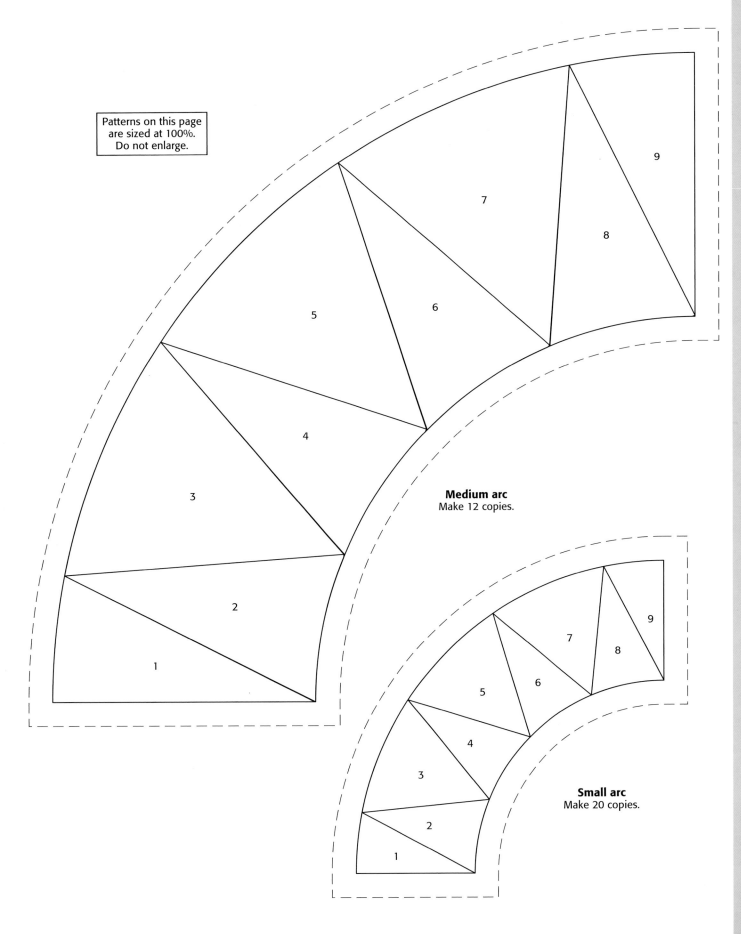

Patterns on this page
are sized at 100%.
Do not enlarge.

Medium arc
Make 12 copies.

Small arc
Make 20 copies.

Quiltmaking Basics

The following pages include some basic information to guide you as you make the projects in this book.

Cutting with Templates

Some projects include pieces that are cut with patterns provided with the specific project instructions. Unless noted otherwise, patterns for piecing include a traditional ¼"-wide seam allowance; appliqué patterns do not include seam allowance. Refer to the project instructions for quantities to cut.

1. Place your preferred template material over the pattern provided. Carefully trace the pattern with a fine-point permanent marker.
2. Cut out the template on the drawn line. If you plan to use the template to cut pieces for fusible appliqué, skip the next two steps and follow the instructions provided by the manufacturer of the fusible product to prepare the appliqués.
3. Place the template on the right side of the fabric. Draw around the template with a water-soluble pen or pencil.
4. If the pattern is for piecing, cut out the fabric shape directly on the drawn line. If the pattern is for appliqué, cut out the fabric shape ¼" beyond the drawn line.

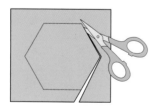

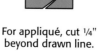

For piecing, cut directly on drawn line. For appliqué, cut ¼" beyond drawn line.

Foundation Piecing

Cut out fabric pieces roughly ¾" larger than the numbered sections they correspond to on the foundation-piecing pattern. Set your machine for a smaller-than-usual stitch length for better needle perforation and to facilitate paper removal later. In the following instructions, the printed side of the pattern is considered the *reverse* or *wrong side* of the pattern.

1. Photocopy the pattern in the quantity indicated in the project instructions.
2. Pin fabric piece 1 wrong side down to section 1 on the unprinted side of the pattern as shown. Hold the pattern up to the light to make sure that section 1 is entirely covered by the fabric.

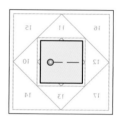

3. Place and pin fabric piece 2 right sides together on top of fabric piece 1 as shown. Check that both pieces extend at least ¼" past their shared sewing line.

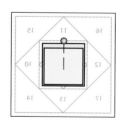

4. Turn the pattern over and sew directly on the line that divides section 1 from section 2 as shown. Start and stop sewing a couple of stitches before and after the sewing line.

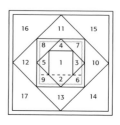

5. Turn the foundation over and finger-press fabric piece 2 open. Hold the pattern up to the light to make sure that both sections 1 and 2 are completely covered by the fabric with enough extra for the seam allowances.

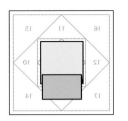

6. Fold fabric 2 back to fabric 1 and trim the seam to ¼" as shown. Press fabric 2 open again.

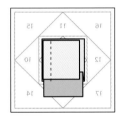

7. Add the appropriate fabric for each succeeding section and repeat steps 3–6 to complete the block.

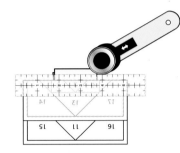

8. Press the completed block and trim along the dotted perimeter lines with a rotary cutter.

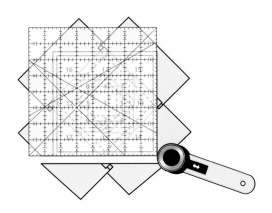

9. Carefully remove the paper pattern. Use tweezers to remove any paper remnants in the seams.

Making Folded Bias Strips

1. Press the fabrics you have chosen for the bias strips (such as vines and stems) and use your rotary cutter to straighten the edges.

2. Align the 45° marking on your ruler with the bottom edge of a straightened piece of fabric from step 1 as shown. Use your rotary cutter to make a cut along the long edge of the ruler on the diagonal (bias) of the fabric as shown.

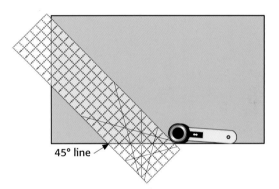

45° line

3. Use the markings on your ruler to cut bias strips in the width designated in the project's cutting instructions. Cut enough strips from the fabric to total the measurement given.

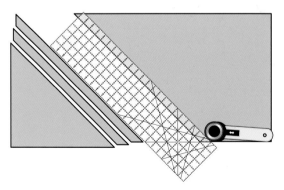

4. To join the strips, place them right sides together, offsetting the angled edge by ¼" as shown. Sew the strips together and press the seams open to reduce the bulk.

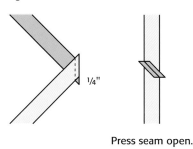

Press seam open.

5. Follow the manufacturer's instructions on the recommended bias-tape maker to make folded bias strips in the required length.

Attaching Borders

It is important to measure your quilt top before adding the borders. Measure through the center rather than along the edges, which might be somewhat distorted due to handling or pressing.

1. Carefully press the center of the quilt top.
2. Place the pressed top on an even surface and smooth flat.
3. Measure the quilt top from top to bottom through the center. Cut the side borders to this measurement.
4. Pin the side borders to the quilt top, first matching the midpoint and then the corners. If necessary, ease the quilt top and the borders to fit. Don't skimp on pins.
5. Sew the side borders to the quilt top. Press the seams toward the borders.

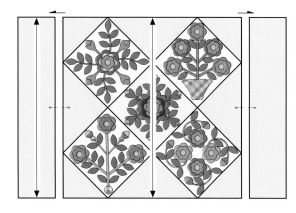

6. Again, place the quilt top on an even surface and smooth flat. Measure the quilt top from side to side, including the side borders just added.
7. Repeat steps 4 and 5 to sew the top and bottom borders to the quilt top; press.

Layering and Basting the Quilt

1. Trim all loose threads from the back of the quilt top, especially dark threads that might show through to the front of the quilt. If hand quilting, trim all the dog-ear triangles to reduce bulk. Carefully press the top.
2. If desired, mark the quilt top with a quilting design of your choice.
3. Piece the backing fabric, if needed, pressing the seams open. Cut the backing at least 2" larger than the quilt top on all sides.
4. Place the backing, wrong side up, on a clean, flat surface and tape it to secure.
5. Cut the batting so it is also 2" larger than the quilt top on all sides. Center the batting on top of the backing. Tape the batting to the basting surface on all sides.
6. Center the quilt top, right side up, on top of the batting and backing. Smooth the top and tape it down on all sides with masking tape.
7. For a long-term hand-quilting project, use light-colored thread and a long needle to baste all three layers together in a 3" to 4" grid.

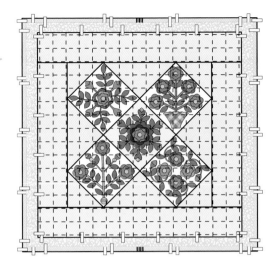

You may substitute stainless steel or rustproof safety pins if the quilt will be completed right away. (Safety pins left in a quilt for a prolonged period may snag or leave holes.) Use safety pins to baste for machine quilting, taking care not to place them in areas you intend to quilt.

8. Trim the batting to approximately 1" beyond the edges of the quilt top.

9. For hand quilting, finish by folding the backing and batting to the front of the quilt and basting in place. This will protect the raw edges from unraveling while the quilt is being handled during quilting.

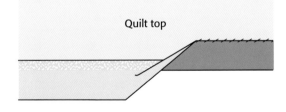

Quilt top

Making and Attaching Binding

1. With right sides together, overlap the ends of two binding strips. Sew the ends as shown. Trim the seam and press open.

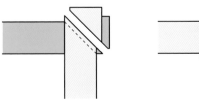

2. Continue sewing the strips together to make the desired length of binding. Fold the binding in half lengthwise, right sides together, and press.

3. Trim the batting and backing even with the quilt top. Straighten the edges and square the corners of the quilt as needed. Line up the raw edges of the binding with the edge of the quilt top. Leave a 6" tail and begin sewing the binding in place with a scant ⅜" seam.

4. Stop sewing ⅜" from the first corner. Remove the quilt from the sewing machine and fold the binding away from the corner at a 90° angle.

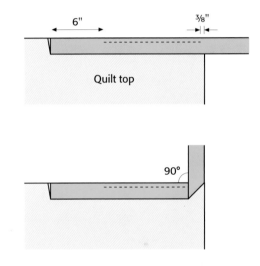

5. Fold the binding back on itself, aligning it with the next side of the quilt. Pin to secure and begin sewing from the edge of the quilt, stopping 3/8" from the next corner. Continue turning corners and sewing the binding to the quilt until you reach a point approximately 12" from where you started sewing.

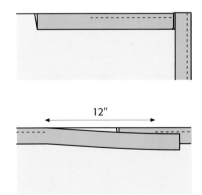

6. Remove the quilt from the sewing machine. Open the folded binding to determine where the ends will meet and pin in place. Fold and finger-press the binding ends away from each other at 90° angles. Trim the binding ends ¼" from the finger-pressed creases.

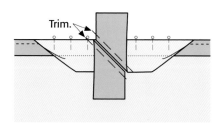

7. Use a ¼" seam allowance to sew the binding ends together. Finger-press the seam open. Refold the binding and finish sewing it to the quilt.
8. Fold the binding to the back of the quilt and hand stitch the folded edge in place using matching thread and small stitches. Occasionally check to make sure the stitches don't show on the front of the quilt.
9. Tuck the binding into itself at the corners and stitch to secure.

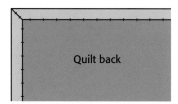

Making and Attaching a Quilt Sleeve

1. Cut a strip of fabric 9" wide x the finished width of the quilt, piecing if necessary.
2. Turn the short raw edges ⅜" to the wrong side and press; repeat. Sew close to the first pressed fold.

3. Fold the strip lengthwise, wrong sides together. Use a ½" seam allowance to sew the long sides of the sleeve. Press the seam open. Trim the ends of the seams at an angle.

4. Center the seam on the sleeve and press.

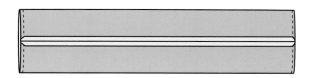

5. Center and pin the sleeve, seam side down, to the back of the quilt, just below the binding. The edges of the sleeve should end approximately ¾" from the outside edges of the quilt. Hand stitch the top pressed edge of the sleeve to the quilt, being careful not to stitch through to the front of the quilt.
6. Pin the sleeve to the quilt back along the lengthwise seam and lift the second pressed edge ½" back toward the binding. Pin and stitch in place. This creates a little fullness to accommodate a quilt hanger and allows the quilt to hang flat. Remove all pins.

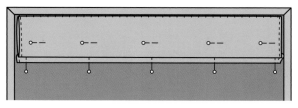

Fold edge of sleeve ½" toward binding.

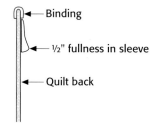

7. Stitch the inside edges of the sleeve to the quilt top, tucking in the trimmed ends of the sleeve seam.

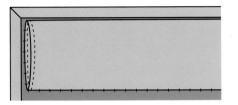

Quilt Labels

Quilt labels can be hand lettered or hand embroidered, stitched on the sewing machine, or created with photo transfers. Whatever method you choose to make them, labels are important for preserving a quilt's history. The more information available about the quilt, the more valuable it will be to its future owners, both sentimentally and financially. Be sure to include the following when documenting a quilt: the name of the quilt and its maker, where the quilt was made, the date the quilt was finished (perhaps, also, the date it was started), the quilt's place in a series if that is appropriate, and the identity of the recipient or the event it commemorates. Attach the finished label to a lower corner of the reverse side of the quilt with small stitches, being careful not to sew through to the front of the quilt.

Always use an indelible pen when writing a label by hand. Press a piece of freezer paper to the wrong side of the label to prevent the fabric from slipping. When the sentiment is complete, press the finished label with a hot dry iron to set the ink.

Resources

Books

Connors, Michael. *Cuban Elegance*. New York: Harry N. Abrams, 2004.

Editors of Harmony Guides. *Knitting Techniques: All You Need to Know About Hand Knitting*. Vol. 1. London: Collins & Brown, 1998.

Editors of *Vogue Knitting* magazine. V*ogue Knitting: The Ultimate Knitting Book*. New York: Sterling Publishing, 2002.

Hopkins, Judy. *Around the Block with Judy Hopkins: 200 Rotary-Cut Blocks in 6 Sizes*. Woodinville, WA: Martingale & Company, 1994.

Parker, Carolyn. *R Is for Rose*. Cincinnati: F + W Publications, 2005.

Phillips, Roger, and Martyn Rix. *Old Roses*. London: Pan Macmillan, 1998.

Wells, Valori. *Radiant New York Beauties: 14 Paper-Pieced Quilt Projects*. Lafayette, CA: C&T Publishing, 2003.

———. *Stitch 'n Flip Quilts: 14 Fantastic Projects*. Lafayette, CA: C&T Publishing, 2000.

Wood, Dorothy. *Rennie Mackintosh: Inspirations in Embroidery*. London: Chrysalis Books Group, 2004.

Products

Bias-tape makers
Clover Needlecraft, Inc.
(562) 282-0200
www.clover-usa.com

Hexagon templates
Item SYW-1½
I Spy 1½" Hexagon and Equilateral Triangle
(800) 982-7326
www.ardcotemplates.com

About the Authors

Catherine and Jennifer

JENNIFER ROUNDS jumped into quilting feet first without tools or significant knowledge of the craft. In her first quilt, she used old record-album covers as templates and pieced chintz florals. She acquired a rotary cutter and a straight edge by the time she made her second quilt, but she used her kitchen cutting board instead of a rotary mat. Jennifer has since become far more sophisticated, and much kinder to her equipment. She designs and makes quilts by commission and includes a major Northern California hospital among her clientele. Jennifer has written the "Feature Teacher" column for *The Quilter* magazine since 1999 and is also a contributor to *Fabric Trends*. *A Dozen Roses* is her fifth quilting title and her third collaboration with Catherine Comyns. Outside of quilting, Jennifer writes feature articles about fitness as well as home and design, does freelance copywriting, and handles domestic policy for her husband, teenage sons, and family dog—she maintains serenity with large doses of ballet and Pilates. Jennifer's favorite rose is 'Peace'.

CATHERINE COMYNS'S first sewing project was a dress for her little sister. A bossy eight-year-old, she plunked her sibling on top of a length of seersucker and traced a pattern for an A-line sheath, which she tacked together with running stitches. Everybody loved her inventiveness, but to her disappointment, there was no runway debut at Sunday services. Undaunted by the mixed reviews, Catherine kept sewing and found a true passion for sewn crafts. Even with a marriage to her high school beau, a career as a neonatal nurse, and raising two daughters, Catherine has always made time for quiltmaking—although part of the attraction is her addiction to the smell of hot pressed cotton infused with her homemade scented sizing. Now retired from nursing and an empty nester, Catherine judges quilt shows and enjoys quilting and knitting for her loved ones. Beyond her crafts, Catherine volunteers for local causes, pursues studies in psychology, French, and yoga, and mothers Phoebe the Wonder Cat. 'Sterling Silver' is her favorite rose.

New and Bestselling Titles from

Martingale®
& COMPANY

America's Best-Loved Craft & Hobby Books®
America's Best-Loved Knitting Books®

That Patchwork Place®

America's Best-Loved Quilt Books®

APPLIQUÉ
Adoration Quilts
Appliqué at Play *NEW!*
Appliqué Takes Wing
Easy Appliqué Samplers
Favorite Quilts
   from Anka's Treasures *NEW!*
Garden Party
Mimi Dietrich's Baltimore Basics *NEW!*
Raise the Roof
Stitch and Split Appliqué
Tea in the Garden

FOCUS ON WOOL
Hooked on Wool
Purely Primitive
Simply Primitive
Warm Up to Wool

GENERAL QUILTMAKING
All Buttoned Up *NEW!*
Alphabet Soup
American Doll Quilts
Calendar Kids *NEW!*
Cottage-Style Quilts
Creating Your Perfect Quilting Space
Creative Quilt Collection Volume One
Dazzling Quilts *NEW!*
Follow the Dots . . . to Dazzling Quilts
Follow-the-Line Quilting Designs
Follow-the-Line Quilting Designs
   Volume Two
Fresh Look at Seasonal Quilts, A *NEW!*
Merry Christmas Quilts
Prairie Children and Their Quilts *NEW!*
Primitive Gatherings
Quilt Revival
Sensational Sashiko
Simple Traditions

LEARNING TO QUILT
Blessed Home Quilt, The
Happy Endings, Revised Edition
Let's Quilt!
Magic of Quiltmaking, The
Quilter's Quick Reference Guide, The
Your First Quilt Book (or it should be!)

PAPER PIECING
40 Bright and Bold Paper-Pieced Blocks
300 Paper-Pieced Quilt Blocks
Easy Machine Paper Piecing
Quilt Block Bonanza
Quilter's Ark, A
Show Me How to Paper Piece
Spellbinding Quilts *NEW!*

PIECING
40 Fabulous Quick-Cut Quilts
101 Fabulous Rotary-Cut Quilts
365 Quilt Blocks a Year: Perpetual Calendar
1000 Great Quilt Blocks
Better by the Dozen
Big 'n Easy
**Border Workbook, 10th Anniversary
   Edition, The** *NEW!*
Clever Quarters, Too *NEW!*
Lickety-Split Quilts
New Cuts for New Quilts *NEW!*
Over Easy
Sew One and You're Done
Simple Chenille Quilts
Snowball Quilts *NEW!*
Stack a New Deck
Sudoku Quilts *NEW!*
Two-Block Theme Quilts
Twosey-Foursey Quilts *NEW!*
Variations on a Theme
Wheel of Mystery Quilts

QUILTS FOR BABIES & CHILDREN
Even More Quilts for Baby
More Quilts for Baby
Quilts for Baby
Sweet and Simple Baby Quilts

SCRAP QUILTS
More Nickel Quilts
Nickel Quilts
Save the Scraps
Scraps of Time
Simple Strategies for Scrap Quilts *NEW!*
Successful Scrap Quilts from
   Simple Rectangles
Treasury of Scrap Quilts, A

CRAFTS
Bag Boutique
Greeting Cards Using Digital Photos
It's a Wrap
Miniature Punchneedle Embroidery
Passion for Punchneedle, A *NEW!*
Scrapbooking Off the Page…and on
   the Wall

KNITTING & CROCHET
365 Knitting Stitches a Year:
   Perpetual Calendar
Crochet from the Heart
Cute Crochet for Kids *NEW!*
First Crochet
First Knits
Fun and Funky Crochet
Funky Chunky Knitted Accessories
Handknit Style II *NEW!*
Knits from the Heart
Knits, Knots, Buttons, and Bows
Knitter's Book of Finishing Techniques, The
Little Box of Crocheted Hats and Scarves,
   The
Little Box of Knitted Throws, The
Little Box of Scarves, The
Modern Classics *NEW!*
Pursenalities
Saturday Sweaters
Sensational Knitted Socks
Silk Knits *NEW!*
Yarn Stash Workbook, The

Our books are available at
bookstores and your favorite
craft, fabric, and yarn retailers.
If you don't see the title
you're looking for, visit us at
www.martingale-pub.com
or contact us at:

1-800-426-3126

International: 1-425-483-3313
Fax: 1-425-486-7596
Email: info@martingale-pub.com